ROUTLEDGE LIBRARY EDITIONS:
AID

Volume 3

THE CONTRADICTIONS OF
FOREIGN AID

THE CONTRADICTIONS OF FOREIGN AID

DESMOND MCNEILL

Routledge
Taylor & Francis Group

LONDON AND NEW YORK

First published in 1981 by Croom Helm Ltd

This edition first published in 2020
by Routledge
2 Park Square, Milton Park, Abingdon, Oxon OX14 4RN

and by Routledge
52 Vanderbilt Avenue, New York, NY 10017

Routledge is an imprint of the Taylor & Francis Group, an informa business

British Library Cataloguing in Publication Data
A catalogue record for this book is available from the British Library

ISBN: 978-0-367-27806-9 (Set)
ISBN: 978-0-429-32859-6 (Set) (ebk)
ISBN: 978-0-367-26247-1 (Volume 3) (hbk)
ISBN: 978-0-429-29226-2 (Volume 3) (ebk)

Publisher's Note
The publisher has gone to great lengths to ensure the quality of this reprint but
points out that some imperfections in the original copies may be apparent.

Disclaimer
The publisher has made every effort to trace copyright holders and would welcome
correspondence from those they have been unable to trace.

The Contradictions of Foreign Aid

Desmond McNeill

CROOM HELM
London & Canberra

© 1981 Desmond McNeill
Croom Helm Ltd, Provident House, Burrell Row,
Beckenham, Kent BR3 1AT
Croom Helm Australia, PO Box 391,
Manuka, ACT 2603, Australia
Reprinted 1983

British Library Cataloguing in Publication Data

McNeill, Desmond
  The contradictions of foreign aid.
  1. Economic assistance
  I. Title
  361.6'172'4   HC60

  ISBN 0-7099-1731-9

Printed and bound in Great Britain by
Professional Books, Abingdon, Oxon

CONTENTS

PREFACE

I have written this book for two reasons: first, because of my dismay at the degree of cynicism which is encountered amongst a large proportion, perhaps even the majority, of those involved in the field of development aid; secondly, because despite acknowledgement, most recently by the Brandt Commission, of the need for a new relationship of equal partnership between donor and recipient countries, I believe that this will not come about until the myths of development aid are finally abandoned.

My purpose is to analyse how development aid actually works in practice, to point out its defects, to identify their causes and, if possible, to offer some hope for improvement. The book is intended for a number of different readers. Those who work in or for aid agencies will recognise much that they already know, but may be persuaded to think more critically and perhaps more constructively about these problems. Those who work in the recipient countries may come to understand more clearly what aid is about, and hence be better equipped to perform their role of 'equal partner' in the aid relationship. Students of development may gain a more real picture of aid than they would find in textbook descriptions. The uncritical layman may come to see that aid is neither simple nor faultless. The critical layman may better understand and sympathise with the problems facing both donor and recipient. The book may appeal less to an academic audience already acquainted with the issues, but I hope it may succeed in its purpose of emphasising the practical realities of aid, and especially the preoccupations of the recipients, without undue sacrifice of academic rigour.

The reader will notice that I make few references to other publications. Most of the examples given to illustrate my arguments are taken from my own experience — although they could have been supplemented many times over by similar examples taken from the experience of others involved in aid with whom I have spoken, or whose books and articles I have read.

I am grateful to Dr Nigel Harris and others at the Development Planning Unit, University College, London who have commented upon parts of the book; to Martin Griffiths for his valuable advice; and to Signe Howell who suggested that I write it, and blended encouragement with criticism in appropriate measure to ensure that I finish it.

THE CONTRADICTIONS OF FOREIGN AID

1 INTRODUCTION

Much that is wrong with foreign aid is caused not by incompetence
or corruption but by the complex machinery which has been
developed to enable aid to be transmitted from donor to recipient.
This machinery has been designed and constructed mainly by the
donors, with the stated intention of making the aid process more
efficient, but it actually causes or exacerbates many of the very
problems that aid is meant to alleviate. This is the subject of this
book.

My purpose is to present a critique of the practice of foreign aid;
to analyse the aid process and who controls it, to investigate the
exercise of leverage by donors, to examine the interests of the
different parties involved, to identify the problems that result, and
to suggest alternatives, based on the foregoing analysis, which may
allow the aid process to operate more effectively in the interest of
those who need it. I am in favour of aid, in principle, but believe
that it can, and must, be improved. The many failures of the system,
which are all too familiar to those involved in the 'aid business'
should more frequently be the subject of open debate. My purpose
in this book is to contribute to such a debate – critically, but, I
hope, constructively.

Foreign aid consists essentially in the people of one country
providing assistance to the people of another country, each being
represented by an agency.[1] It is a rather curious phenomenon which
can be traced back, in its present form, only 20 or 30 years – to
the period of the Cold War and the emergence of a sudden rash
of independent nations. As I shall explain in Chapter 4, the reasons
why aid is given are numerous and confused. To some extent aid
is intended to benefit the people of the donor country rather than
the recipients, and the donor exercises leverage so as to induce
the recipient to act in certain ways favourable to the donor's own

interest. In addition, the donor country does not always trust the
recipient agency to act in the best interests of the people it
represents — whether through incompetence or self-seeking — and
may therefore try to exercise another form of leverage in order to
control or influence the recipient country's actions.

The nature of the aid process is to a large extent determined by
the need of the donor to exercise such leverage. But also of importance, both to the nature and the outcome of the aid process,
are the concerns of all the various parties involved: the civil servants
and politicians of donor and recipient countries, the contractors,
consultants and advisers. The pursuance of their interests may not
result in the best outcome for the intended beneficiaries of aid, so
that the flow of aid is still further diverted from its optimal path.

In this introductory chapter I will focus attention on two
particular issues which exemplify much that is wrong with the
present practice. These are so commonplace in the experience of
aid donors as to frequently escape mention. Yet they are of crucial
significance, and, to the uninitiated, may appear almost incredible.
The first is the fact that although the volume of aid provided is
manifestly insufficient to make a major impact on development,
one of the biggest problems facing donor agencies is how to spend
the little money they are allocated. (This is known in the jargon as a
problem of 'absorptive capacity'.) The second, related to the first,
is the fact that a major criterion of success of an aid agency is
simply its ability to get money spent. These two facts alone should
be sufficient to induce aid donors to look very critically at the
way in which they give aid, and to wonder whether it can possibly
be correct. In view of the importance of these two points I must
elaborate further on them.

There is ample evidence that aid agencies find it difficult to
spend their budgets. First, there are continual complaints by donors
that they cannot identify enough projects; secondly, the projects
proposed by recipients are often 'too small' for funding agencies;
and thirdly, some donors actively encourage recipients to spend
money more quickly.

Reports of aid agencies often refer to the problem of absorptive
capacity, and various measures are recommended for alleviating it.
The Brandt Commission, for example, propose 'more purposeful

technical assistance to identify, prepare and implement projects, and to help operate plants and installations already established'.[2] To the outsider, however, the very concept is remarkable — that a major problem in development aid is to get the money spent.

Further evidence of the same point is the keen competition which arises between different aid agencies seeking good projects in the same country. I have witnessed missions representing two bilateral agencies in hot competition for a particularly desirable water supply project. A similar situation arises within the UN system. As the Jackson Report suggests: 'what exists today is "inter-agency rivalry" for projects'.[3]

Finally I would refer to the common practice among aid donors of 'ventriloquising' aid requests from prospective recipients i.e. encouraging them to ask for specific projects of the donor's choosing. Again the Jackson Report provides a relevant quotation: 'At present the greatest difficulty lies in the fact that far too many project requests are drafted by agency salesmen.'[4]

The fact that projects proposed by countries are often regarded as too small is more difficult to document since such views are generally only expressed in the preliminary meeting with aid missions, or exchanges of letters about specific project requests. But in view of the high fixed cost of organising an appraisal mission, writing reports, drafting agreements, etc., not to mention the time involved, it is not surprising that donor agencies often prefer to consider one large project, or at least a 'project package' rather than a number of small ones.

The third point, that donors actively encourage recipients to spend money faster, is demonstrated by two facts. The first is that donors such as the World Bank draw up detailed timetables for project implementation, failure to adhere to which can lead to delays in further disbursement of funds. The second is that donors often include technical assistance components in their projects in order to ensure rapid and efficient implementation. The quotation from the Brandt Report confirms this point.

All this is not necessarily foolish, but it certainly appears paradoxical. Such contradictions are indicative of the shortcomings of the present system — which will become more manifest in Chapter 4, which is concerned with the practical problems of aid.

The second issue to which I drew attention is the tendency for aid programmes to be judged largely by their ability to use money quickly. In view of the difficulty of getting funds spent, which I have just described, this is perhaps not surprising. But there is another factor of importance. This is the lack of appropriate criteria for judging performance. How is one to compare the benefits of a project which resulted in the construction of a new road, with another to reduce pest damage to crops, a third which built cattle dips and a fourth which provided educational advisers? In the first case it may be possible to both estimate and evaluate the benefits — although this would not be easy. In the second case one might, perhaps, be able to estimate the number of birds killed and value the crops saved. In the third case the number of dips built could easily be measured — but what if they are not used, or the dip fluid is not available? And in the fourth case the problem of evaluation is insoluble.

In such circumstances it is not surprising that money — the only element that is invariably quantifiable (and also common to all projects) — acquires a disproportionate significance as a measure of performance. Donor agencies, therefore, find that their standards are assessed largely in terms of their ability to spend money, and that one of their biggest problems is to find suitable ways of using the budget they are allocated.

This creates an environment conducive to cynicism and wastage. Yet there are many people involved in aid who are well intentioned and genuinely concerned to improve the lot of the inhabitants of developing countries. These people gradually become disillusioned with aid — not generally because they come to doubt the purity of the motives behind it, nor because they find themselves surrounded by fools and villains, but because however hard they try, and however desirable may be their objectives, the structure within which they operate, and the rules which govern and restrict them, seem to distort and nullify their actions. Some leave the aid business, some remain and enjoy the material benefits that it provides. Most are disenchanted and bemoan the fact that aid so seldom achieves what is expected of it. My hope in this book is that some of those who are disenchanted may be encouraged to look again, more critically and analytically, at what is wrong with aid, and to realise that little can be done without radically changing the way in which the process works.

Notes

1. Unless otherwise stated, and in particular in reference to statistical data, I adopt the definition of aid used by the Development Assistance Committee of the OECD:

> The word 'aid' or 'asssistance' refers only to flows which qualify as 'official development assistance' (ODA) i.e. grants or loans:
>> undertaken by the official sector;
>> with promotion of economic development and welfare as main objectives;
>> at concessional financial terms (if a loan, at least 25 per cent grant element).
>
> In addition to financial flows, technical co-operation is included in aid. It comprises grants (and a very small volume of loans) to nationals of developing countries receiving education or training at home or abroad, and to defray the costs of teachers, administrators, advisers and similar personnel serving in developing countries.

Development Co-operation, DAC Review 1979 (OECD, Paris, 1979).

2. *North—South: A Programme for Survival*, Report for the Independent Commission on International Development Issues (Pan Books, London, 1980).

3. United Nations, *A Study of the Capacity of the United Nations Development System* (UN, Geneva, 1969).

4. Ibid.

2 THE AID PROCESS

Introduction

In this chapter I shall summarise the nature of the aid process as it currently operates, and demonstrate the extent to which the 'rules of the game' are determined by the aid donors.

Before beginning, let us consider what the aid process could or should be like. It must be such as to allow resources to flow from one group of people, represented by an agency, to another group of people, also represented by an agency. In such a process there are a number of decisions to be taken which may be summarised as follows: How much aid in total is to be provided, what is to be the share of each recipient country, and to what uses will the resources be put in each case? The aid process should obviously be such as to ensure that the outcome of these decisions leads to an efficient and equitable allocation. What this means in practice is difficult to say since despite the hopes of economists such a judgement is largely subjective.

In some cases the problem of how to assess and compare the relative needs of prospective recipients hardly arises. Where aid is provided as a quid pro quo, the precise use to which it is put is not of major significance to the donor. Ironically, the recipient government is then allowed a fairly free hand in deciding how it will be spent. But what of the aid which is actually intended to benefit the recipients?

It used to be thought that the answer to the allocation problem lay in cost-benefit analysis. Armies of economists would prepare and appraise 'shelves' of projects for each sector in every country. All those with high rates of return (above a certain minimum threshold) would be financed. Experience has shown that the necessary armies do not exist, and the shelves are therefore empty. It has also cast doubt on whether such a method would work even if it were applied, since there is more to the effective use of foreign aid than rate of return calculations.

Yet some of the legend lingers on. There is a view that the answer to many of the problems of foreign aid lies simply in increasing sophistication: more and better planning, project preparation and appraisal. Factors other than technical and economic are understood as important — but the solution in all cases is seen as more experts and more studies. Running counter to this is a desire that recipient countries should become more self-sufficient, and that the role of the aid donors should be to support rather than to replace them in their efforts to achieve development. The rather unhappy compromise that has resulted is that recipients have the appearance of taking many of the decisions, while in practice the donors retain considerable control, by means of a complex set of procedures and regulations. It appears that, in the final analysis, donors are not prepared to transfer full control over the allocation of aid resources from themselves to the recipients. They seek to exert influence, as I shall show in Chapter 3, over most stages of the decision-making process.

Obviously the precise nature of the aid process varies between different agencies, and what I shall now describe is not of universal application. In particular, it is important to distinguish between bilateral and multilateral donor agencies in some parts of the process. Apart from this, however, there is sufficient uniformity for the description that follows to be generally applicable.

The first point to note is that aid does not 'flow' but rather consists of a number of discrete 'lumps'. It is sometimes the case that countries receive general budgetary support on a periodic basis, but more commonly resources have to be earmarked for specific programmes or projects. The process of allocating resources to these projects and programmes involves three decisions: what is to be the total volume of aid; how is this to be shared between recipient countries; and to what use will the aid be put?

The Total Volume of Aid

The total volume of aid to be provided is decided by the govern-

ments of the donor countries. Their decisions will be influenced
mainly by the current state of the economy, the international
climate of opinion amongst donors, and the relative power of the
minister responsible for aid. Prospective recipients, as a group, have
little power to increase the amount. The statistics in Appendix 1
show how much different donors give, expressed as a percentage of
their gross national product. The figures for OECD countries
average only about 0.35 per cent, and for the Soviet Union and
other Comecon countries apparently less than 0.1 per cent, while
some Arab oil-exporting countries have been far more generous,
with figures ranging from 6 per cent to 15 per cent in recent years.

In the short term the major determinant is in fact the amount
of the previous year's budget. As Judith Hart, former Minister of
Overseas Development (now ODA) in Britain records of her
experience in the Ministry:

> The only important policy decision left to the cabinet was the
> decision on volume, and that decision was set in a context in
> which the cabinet, bereft of clear and evolving policy objectives,
> was as likely as not to say 'the same as last year', for want of a
> case to justify another figure.[1]

The Share Received by Different Countries

Donor countries must decide not only how much each country
should receive, but also how much to allocate to multilateral
agencies. Practice varies widely between countries, so that while
France contributed only 13 per cent of its total aid funds to multilateral agencies (in 1979), Finland and Italy contributed over half.
The opportunities for exerting leverage to the donor's advantage
are obviously reduced by channelling funds via multilateral agencies.
Other considerations are the capacity of the bilateral aid agency to
disburse funds, and the reputation of the multilateral agencies for
spending their funds well.

The decision as to how to share bilateral aid funds between
different recipient countries is not wholly separate from this
decision, since geographical preferences can also be expressed by

favouring certain regional banks. (Thus the Japanese, for example, are major contributors to the Asian Development Bank, and the USA to the Inter-American Development Bank.) It is hard to discover the rationale behind the inter-country allocation of aid on a world scale. Former dependencies are obviously favoured, not only by France and Britain, but also the Netherlands (Indonesia), Belgium (Congo), Italy (Somalia) and Australia (Papua New Guinea). Strategic and commercial considerations also play a major part. Attempts have been made to discern some underlying pattern in the overall aid flows, and to test whether the poorest countries are given special attention, but an analysis carried out in the mid-1960s found that the only significant factor appeared to be the size of the recipient country's population. 'If one attempts to "fit" an equation to this general dictum, the conclusion would be that on average for the period 1964 to 1966 every recipient country received per year a basic amount of about $21 million plus $2 per head of population as bilateral official aid.'[2] Clearly this is to the relative disadvantage of the larger countries, most notably India.

Donor countries generally operate on the basis of a forward budget of about five years for their aid programmes. The problem of reconciling an annual budgetary procedure with this need for longer term planning is dealt with in various ways. Thus in Britain the ODA, on the basis of its four year 'aid framework', may agree with a recipient country to provide specified sums over several years, although the funds have not actually been voted by Treasury. Australia operates a rather complex system whereby the executive is allowed to commit bilateral aid funds up to a percentage of the current year's total, the percentage declining to only 10 per cent for four years in the future. Germany is perhaps the most stringent, with the requirement that future commitments be formally authorised by the *Bundestag*.

Donors will generally prepare country reports at least for their major beneficiaries, describing the performance and prospects of their economies. But the overriding tendency here also is for allocations to be on a 'same as last year' basis, barring wars or major changes of government. Not only is there a shortage of the information necessary to make an appropriate judgement on the merits of the case, but the criteria for decision are also all too often lacking. To quote again from Judith Hart:

> I remember that at the first meeting in my time at ODM to
> discuss the 'aid framework', as it is called, in January 1970, at
> which the heads of the main departments of the Ministry were
> present, I asked what the criteria had been. I received almost
> as many answers as there were people present.[3]

Before concluding this section I must discuss the inter-country
allocation of funds by the multilateral agencies. Whereas their total
budgets are determined by the amounts that individual countries
choose to give, the agencies have the power to decide where to
spend these funds. The banks are bound by their mandates to
apply 'sound banking principles', in disbursing their funds, and each
regional bank is required to concentrate on its particular geographic
area. Within these limits they all try to achieve some sort of
balance in their allocations on a *per capita* basis. The specialised
agencies (UNESCO, WHO, ILO, FAO etc.) are sectoral rather than
regional in their specialisation, so that the decision by donor
countries as to which to support affects the sectoral allocation of
funds (although this relationship is rather blurred, since there are
considerable areas of overlap between agencies).

The multilateral agencies also operate on the basis of forward
budgets of about five years. The inter-country allocation of funds
is not, of course, independent of pressures from individual donor
countries, and indeed certain special contributions to agencies are
made by donors on the understanding that they will be spent on
specific projects. In these decisions the power of the prospective
recipients is very small. In the case of the banks, the role of the
professional becomes particularly important since allocations have to
be justified on the basis of rational principles of appraisal and assessment. The specialised agencies generally seek to obtain the involvement of the prospective recipients to a greater degree, but more
with regard to the content of their country's programme than its
magnitude.

How the Aid is Used

So far the aid donors have, in effect, taken all the decisions. The last stage in the process is to determine how the funds are to be used. In terms of time, effort and cost this stage is the most important. Broadly, the decision is taken neither by the donor nor the recipient but by a combination of the two. The myth is that the recipients prepare and propose projects for financing, and the donors select those they favour. The reality is that many of the proposals come from the donors, who are actively involved in the preparation of projects. They also specify the rules regarding what sorts of aid may be given and in what way, rules which are relatively inflexible and which, as I shall later show, have certain counter-productive effects.

In order to establish how the process works, I begin with the recipient side. Here, the key documents are the Development Plan and the Annual Budget, both of which deserve some discussion.

Virtually every developing country prepares a Plan — a remarkable fact in view of their considerable uniformity and the notable absence of such plans in the West. This may be attributable to what Myrdal called the 'ideology of planning' or, more cynically, one may simply regard the preparation of a Plan as a prerequisite for obtaining aid. Certainly the form in which plans are prepared owes much to the requirements of foreign aid donors (and indeed they are often prepared with technical assistance from abroad). Capital programmes and projects are listed by ministry, their costs broken down into local and foreign cost components and phased over the Plan period. The gap between the total expenditure on these and the estimated revenue available for capital programmes is assumed to be covered by foreign aid. The magnitude of this gap is necessarily rather arbitrary since it depends on the amount of aid that donors are prepared to provide. Since the donors do not commit themselves far in advance, and prefer, in any case, that Plans are not predicated on the assumption that massive support will be provided from abroad, the calculations for planning purposes tend also to be made on a 'same as last year' basis.

It is not sufficient for the Plan simply to identify the shortfall between their revenue and expenditure. Aid donors are interested in certain types of projects, and within those projects they will finance only certain parts. Recurrent costs, as I shall discuss later, are not generally financed by aid donors, and as a result the Plan often pays scant attention to this aspect of budgeting. At worst, a Development Plan consists simply of a bland set of unexceptionable aspirations followed by unrealistic forecasts of funds available for investment and a shopping list of projects arbitrarily phased over the period of the Plan, and inadequately costed. At best, it may be a document which many Western countries would find it hard to emulate. Either way it tends to assume considerable importance in the eyes of the aid donor, to whom it represents the most authoritative and detailed statement of government policy available.

For the recipient country, however, the Annual Budget is of more immediate importance. Control over the purse strings is the ultimate power, and this is embodied in the budget, not the Plan. True, inclusion in the budget may be, at least nominally, dependent on prior inclusion in the Plan, but even so this is never a sufficient condition. The process of allocating funds is of course very complex, depending as it does on the relative bargaining power of the different ministries and others involved. The main point of relevance to this book is that a project for which foreign aid funds are assured has an extremely good chance of being included in the budget against possibly better projects which are locally funded. If a donor agency approaches a line ministry with the promise of aid for a specific project this may well be sufficient to guarantee its inclusion in the budget. If the project has already been formally agreed by the government then inclusion in the annual budget is virtually guaranteed, even if other projects are being savagely cut as the result of budgetary problems.

We may therefore contrast the Plan, which is very much an international document, and considerably influenced by the preferences of aid donors, with the Annual Budget which is a more domestic document reflecting the day-to-day problems of financial management. Nevertheless, even the budget is subject to considerable influence by the donor community.

I now turn to the donor side of the process. Apart from doing their 'homework', donor agencies will also send out missions to visit prospective recipient countries. Some of these will, of course, be to review progress on current projects or, perhaps, simply to provide background material for preparing a country report. I shall focus attention on the project identification mission, whose purpose is to find projects which may be suitable for funding. Such a mission will set off with a fair idea of how much money is likely to be available. Guidelines on other matters, such as which types of project or sector to favour may be less well defined both because the criteria for selection of projects are frequently unclear, as already mentioned, and because the reasons for which foreign aid is given are often confused, as I shall discuss in Chapter 4. Nevertheless, multilateral agencies in particular often have an outline allocation between sectors, and even types of project, before the identification mission sets out. The composition of the team can, in this respect, be rather important. If an agricultural expert is included then an agricultural project will probably be found. An engineer, by contrast, may not favour a particular sector but is likely to identify very different types of project from, say, a manpower specialist.

On arrival, the mission will see its local representative. This may merely be a Second Secretary in the Embassy, or in the case of the major donors, there may be a large full-time agency staff. In the latter case the role of the visiting mission is rather modified. USAID (United States Agency for International Development), for example, have about forty resident missions, some with large staffs, enjoying a fair degree of autonomy. Britain has several regional Development Divisions, each covering a number of countries and with power to approve financial commitments up to a specified ceiling. Multilateral agencies are generally well represented. Typically the permanent UN mission, headed by the Resident Representative, includes representatives of WHO, FAO and other agencies as well. A few countries have a permanent World Bank office, the regional banks are beginning to set up more subsidiary offices, and the European Development Fund has representatives in most of the Lome Convention countries.

Having received a briefing from the embassy or local office, the mission may also visit the UN Resident Representative or his assistant, and possibly other bilateral agencies, depending on their area of interest. They will also read a number of documents about the country, of which the most dog-eared will be the World Bank country report, followed, perhaps by the UN country programme.

All this constitutes what may be called the international briefing. It will be supplemented by more informal discussions, in hotel lobbies or at cocktail parties, with other visiting missions, or expatriate advisers and consultants.

Concurrently, the mission will receive a local briefing, meeting first with the Ministry of Foreign Affairs, Development Planning, or Treasury. In case they have not already received it, the mission will then be given a copy of the Development Plan. It is at this stage that the aid process on the donor side begins to 'mesh' with the process on the recipient side. In the next few days, or possibly weeks, possibilities will begin to turn into commitments, as the long, slow, almost irreversible process of project preparation, appraisal, agreement and implementation begins.

Although the precise nature of the decision-making process varies from one agency to another and from one country to another, the stage must necessarily be reached where the donor begins to enter into a commitment. It is most visible, and perhaps most typical, at this point, where the visiting mission begins its tentative and often rather secretive task of deciding what specific programmes or projects it wants to assist. The recipient country is generally eager to oblige with ideas, while the donor mission is faced with the problem of how to spend its funds rapidly and well, without wishing to commit itself too early to a project which may turn out to be ill-chosen.

The process is further complicated by the distinction that must be drawn between line ministries and the 'senior' ministry — whether this be the Treasury or the Ministry of Planning. The line ministries are generally very eager to suggest or agree to projects which the donor agency may wish to finance, whereas the Treasury is likely to be more discriminating, both with regard to the terms and conditions attached to the aid and to the sectors favoured. Donor agencies will have discussions with line ministries about possible projects and may then present the Treasury with what is virtually a *fait accompli*. The extent to which this is possible depends of course on the relative power of the 'senior' ministry, but this can often be quite limited.

In the short period of the mission's stay discussions rapidly merge into negotiations. Perhaps the mission arrives with a very clear mandate and can identify a possible project within a very short time. Perhaps they are subjected to extreme pressure from the President or some other important minister, and find it hard to resist agreeing to the project of their choice. In any event they will soon have to be in a position to discuss the next stage. If the exercise of leverage is a major consideration (as discussed in the next chapter) then negotiations may be quite tough. The aid may be dependent on a specific quid pro quo from the recipient country, or there may be terms attached to it which are unacceptable to the ministry concerned (such as land reforms). But frequently the negotiations are carried out as between benefactor and beneficiary, with the former eager to oblige, but cautious about over-commitment, and the latter also eager to oblige, and wishing to hurry up the process as much as possible. Discussions are then concerned largely with details such as starting dates and counterpart contributions rather than repayment terms, or the possibility of financing recurrent costs. Such issues are usually presented as agency policy and not subject to negotiation.

Formal agreements will eventually be signed, but the disbursement of funds will probably not begin until much more detailed project preparation work has been carried out. This may involve consultants, financed by the donor agency, who are required to plan the project in detail and appraise its feasibility. By the time this stage has been completed donors are extremely loth to back out, so that even if the appraisal points to a negative conclusion, the project is unlikely to be stopped, although it may be heavily modified.

Implementation and Follow-up

With regard to the implementation of a project, practice varies considerably according to the nature of the scheme and the donor agency. At one extreme, there is the 'turn-key operation'. This requires the minimum amount of discussion with and involvement of the recipient country. The construction of a bridge provides an example. The donor employs a firm to prepare detailed designs and to supervise construction, which is carried out by another firm of contractors (probably also from the donor country).

At the other extreme, particularly exemplified by aid from specialised UN agencies, there are programmes more wide-ranging in nature where a number of foreign personnel are attached to the project and closely involved in its day-to-day administration. The Project Manager is probably an expatriate, with a counterpart local officer working with him. The capital component in such a project is generally much less.

In between these two extremes are a range of possibilities. Typically, a large part of the funds provided by the donor will be spent on machinery, equipment and personnel from abroad. Selection of suppliers for these may be the joint responsibility of donor and recipient, but in the case of bilateral aid the power of the recipient is likely to be only nominal.

At all events, there are numerous stages to be gone through: detailed designs, preparation of bills of quantities, putting out to tender, selection of contractors and suppliers, opening of letters of credit, disbursement of funds, supervision of work, accounting and reporting, etc. All these are lengthy procedures, especially as they will, to varying extents, involve the donor agency which, if it has no staff on the ground, will rely on communication by letter, cable and telex.

The follow-up stage, after completion of the project, should include evaluation. This has long been recognised as one of the least satisfactory aspects. Neither donor nor recipient has an interest in criticising its own projects, and drawing attention to its failures.

Even when, as in the case of the UN Joint Inspection Unit, for example, there is a section specifically charged with the task of evaluating selected projects, the representatives of the recipient country are often unwilling openly to voice their criticisms. Whether this is due to good manners, a fear that it would reflect badly on themselves, or that it might reduce the likelihood of more aid, is unclear, but such reticence is not conducive to an improvement in the situation.

An added difficulty is that expectations of projects are almost invariably too high. Myrdal refers to a 'systematic optimistic bias' among leaders and public officials in South Asia when engaged in preparing plans.[4] This is exacerbated by a similar bias on the part of donor agencies. Project proposals are written in glowing terms, timetables for implementation are too optimistic, and the extent of benefits is often exaggerated. Many projects are successful, and bring considerable benefits, but they cannot often match up to their expectations, and such comparisons are all too rarely undertaken or publicised by the agencies responsible.

A discussion of the follow-up stage should also include mention of the fate of the project after the donor agency's input has ceased. In the case of a new bridge this stage is reached immediately on completion, but other less capital-biased projects may involve a donor presence and financial support extending over several years. At the end of this time, such projects may suffer a severe shock when they are suddenly expected to stand on their own feet. Funds perhaps become short, interest in the project wanes, and new aid schemes attract attention elsewhere. This can be a difficult stage to survive successfully. There is an almost inevitable contrast between performance with aid and performance without it, which can act as a further disincentive to the recipient country to undertake a critical evaluation.

Conclusion

Having analysed the four major stages in the aid process which I identified at the outset let me now return to the question of the extent to which these are controlled by the donors. With regard to the total volume of aid to be provided the recipient countries have no effective power whatever. With regard to the amount of aid that each country receives they have the power to refuse but little opportunity to increase the allocation, except by proposing ways in which the funds may be used which they know will gain favour with the donors. Nor are they necessarily informed as to what allocation is planned in future years. With regard to the use to which the aid is put their influence is still limited. They can refuse certain projects and request others, but the rules of the game, which are laid down mainly by the aid donors, allow the donors to exercise considerable leverage over the recipients, as I shall describe in the next chapter.

Such leverage is not always and necessarily detrimental, nor do the donor countries invariably exercise it. My purpose at this stage is not to criticise the nature of the aid process but simply to demonstrate its length and complexity and the extent to which it is determined by the donors. But in Chapter 5 I shall identify a number of problems encountered in aid which may be attributed to the nature of this process.

Notes

1. Judith Hart, *Aid and Liberation* (Victor Gollancz, London, 1973).
2. *Development Assistance: Efforts and Policies of the Members of the Development Assistance Committee*, DAC Review, 1969 (OECD, Paris, 1969).
3. Hart, *Aid and Liberation*.
4. Gunnar Myrdal, *Asian Drama* (Penguin, Harmondsworth, 1968).

3 LEVERAGE

By leverage I mean the use of aid to seek to bring about compliance of the recipient with some form of action favoured by the donor. This chapter is about leverage: what it is, how it is used and what are its effects. It is of importance in an analysis of the aid process not only because the machinery of aid is, in some respects, designed in order to allow leverage to be exercised, but also because some of the problems of aid which I shall be discussing may be attributed to the use of leverage by the donor.

One way in which a country can attempt to influence the policies of another is by promising to provide, or threatening to withold financial or material assistance. Such leverage may be exercised not only in the direct interest of the donor but for other reasons also, as I shall describe. It may be exercised by multilateral donor agencies as well as by individual countries. My definition of the term is therefore deliberately a wide one. The expression is usually regarded as pejorative, and aid donors are increasingly unwilling to state how they exercise leverage, or indeed that they do so at all.

In my analysis I shall distinguish four different ways in which leverage may be exercised: first, to discriminate between countries; secondly, within a country, between different sectors or regions; thirdly, between different projects; and finally, control can be sought over the way in which a project is carried out.

I shall also distinguish three different motives for exerting leverage. The first is self-interest: a desire on the donor's part to induce the recipient to take some action favourable to the recipient's interest (generally political, strategic or economic). The second is a concern with the interests of the people of the recipient country which moves the donor to try and induce the recipient to pursue more equitable and liberal policies. There is, in addition, a third possible objective: to stimulate efficiency and good management on the part of the recipient. This is always stated by donor agencies as being in the interests of the recipient (and hence classifiable under my second category). Recipient countries, however, may regard this motive as ideologically biased (and hence better classified under my first category). I shall discuss the issue below, and at this stage simply distinguish this as a third category.

Two questions may be asked with regard to each method of applying leverage and each motive: is such leverage actually applied; and, what effect does it have? I shall discuss these in turn, followed by a consideration of the more subjective question of whether such leverage should be applied. In order to simplify the presentation I shall defer discussion of the distinction between bilateral and multilateral agencies until later in the chapter.

Donor Self-interest

The first question is thus whether leverage is applied at country level to try and induce recipients to follow courses of action favourable to the donor's interest. The answer is unequivocally yes. Indeed this is perhaps the most common interpretation of the meaning of the term.

Strategic interests represent the most clear-cut example. Thus American aid was provided to Spain, Morocco and Tunisia in exchange for permission to site military bases in these countries.

Political support may also be purchased by sufficient financial assistance. French aid to former African colonies used to be provided on the explicit understanding that France would be consulted before these countries voted at the United Nations on major issues.

Commercial considerations come more into play at sectoral or project level. Although donor countries sometimes seek specific actions by recipient countries which would further their own commercial interests, a more significant phenomenon is the general tendency for a donor country to favour aid to those with which it has, or hopes to develop, strong trading ties. Recent policy statements suggest that British aid will now be a good example. This, however, is only in the loosest sense of the term to be called leverage.

Countries may seek a quid pro quo of a different kind. Thus, the United States provided aid to Turkey in the expectation that the authorities there would reduce the amount of marijuana being produced (and largely smuggled to the USA). Britain attempted, unsuccessfully, to block a World Bank loan to Tanzania because Tanzania was refusing to pay the pensions of former civil servants in the Colonial Service.

What effect does such leverage have? Generally, it causes the recipient country to act as required by the donor. Where there is a specific quid pro quo it is usually evident that this is so. Indeed, if it were not, then the flow of aid would immediately cease. In other cases, for example where political allegiance is being bought, it may be more difficult to ensure that the bargain is kept. The implications of keeping the bargain vary widely. Thus, by reducing marijuana production incomes are reduced; a military base will generate employment in the area, but may also stimulate conflict. Unlike most other forms of leverage, however, this most stark variety, which represents, in a sense, a sale of sovereignty by the recipient, has minimal distorting effects on the economy.

I turn now to the sectoral or regional level. In certain circumstances, leverage is applied to discriminate between sectors within a country in order to further the donor's self-interest. Japanese aid, for example, is heavily concentrated on utilities, especially transport, since this is likely to stimulate exports from their domestic producers. (Japan is a rather special case since much aid results from the initiatives of private Japanese firms preparing and actively promoting specific projects.)

It is important not to confuse this with the common practice of many bilateral aid donors of concentrating on sectors in which they have a particular expertise: the Norwegians in fisheries or shipping; the Dutch in land reclamation; the Danes in agriculture. Such discrimination is not exercised in the donor's interest and should be regarded not as leverage but as intelligent division of labour — although it too can lead to distortions.

A specific sector or region may be chosen in order to please an individual politician or powerful group in the recipient country. Thus the Minister of Industry might be favoured by aid to his sector, or a racial minority assisted by aid to their locality. An individual would rarely merit such treatment, unless he is a budding president, nor is it generally in the donor's interest to favour a minority group. This is therefore less common.

More important is leverage exerted at the project level, to which I now turn. Commercial interests are clearly better served by specifying the project rather than simply the sector, and in order to favour a politically powerful individual, it may be more effective to finance a project in his electorate rather than his Ministry. A new metro might be financed not because it is economically feasible, but because such a project is in the commercial interest of the donor. A massive and continuing quantity of funds will have to be spent on equipment, probably imported from the donor country.

Aid from Eastern Europe and Russia is very largely provided for industrial projects, with the expectation that this will generate exports. (In fact the terms of these loans are generally too hard to allow them to be classified as aid.) Thus, a plant for producing prefabricated housing was provided to a country in South Asia on relatively soft terms. The donor soon proposed an expansion of the plant, but with the additional equipment and expertise provided on even less concessional terms.

The effect of exerting such leverage at both sectoral (or regional) and project level is at best to distort the pattern of development, and at worst to cause direct waste of money and manpower. If there is not a senior ministry with real control over all aid requests, aid donors can quite easily enlist the support of the ministry that will benefit from the prospective project in pressing for its acceptance by the government. Even if the Treasury (or other ministry) has effective power, it will find it hard to resist an offer of aid for a specific project or sector when it cannot confidently assume that a refusal would lead to the selection of a more acceptable project.

In some cases the result will be that the order of priority of a programme is changed, with only slight cost in money terms. Thus, a new water supply is financed for the Minister of Finance's electorate. This is perhaps not the first priority, but nevertheless among the top ten. In other cases, there may be a gross waste of money. The metro, for example, may be not only more expensive than it would have been if imported from another country (even taking into account the concessional terms) but not economically viable in any case. The exercise of leverage to discriminate betweeen sectors, regions or projects, in the interest of the donor, undoubtedly leads to considerable distortions and consequent wastage of resources.

Lastly, under this heading, I consider the question of leverage applied with regard to the actual implementation of the project. The practice of specifying where equipment or materials should be imported from (or 'procurement tying' as it is called) has, quite rightly, received much attention, and this is one of the few areas where quantitative data exist relating to the deleterious effect of aid practice. According to one source,[1] studies have shown that the total increase in costs that results from this practice offen exceeds 20 per cent, and in a much quoted study relating to twenty projects in Pakistan it was concluded that 'the weighted average price (of "tied goods") was 51 per cent higher than under conditions of open competitive bidding.'[2]

Clearly the interest of the donor is served by this system, which imposes other costs also on the recipient country. A related practice which has recently developed is the use of so-called 'mixed credits', which are, in effect, a means of using aid to subsidise exports. A French firm selling diesel generators, for example, applies to the French aid agency to provide assistance to a Third World government which is a prospective purchaser. If the donor agency agrees, the country concerned is then offered the goods at a heavily subsidised price, and the discount is classified as aid. Although accounting for only a small proportion of aid at present, this practice appears to be growing, as domestic recession makes the competition for export markets keener.

The Interest of the Recipient

Many donors exert leverage not for their own self-interest but for that of the people of the recipient country — seeking to encourage social justice by providing or withholding aid. Implicit in this is the judgement that the recipient government is too illiberal or too ill-advised to pursue such policies themselves. The importance of equity considerations in determining the allocation of funds between countries is often referred to in official statements by aid agencies, and in recent years the policy of 'aid to the poorest' has been stressed by most donors, and taken to imply not only emphasis on poor countries, but also on those which are seen to pursue equitable policies which will benefit the lower income groups.

This is often cited as one reason why Tanzania has been particularly favoured. Nyerere's brand of 'African socialism' has a wide appeal, and donors such as Denmark, Norway and Finland have chosen Tanzania as one of their 'countries of concentration'. One could easily point to totalitarian regimes, however, which give scant regard to social justice while receiving large quantities of aid from a range of donors.

The effect at country level is probably very slight. The withholding of aid, accounting for less than 2 per cent of the recipient country's national income in most cases, is unlikely to achieve liberalisation in a reluctant regime. (Clearly the withholding of military assistance, or the case of countries such as Jordan, Mauritania or Reunion where aid accounts for over 20 per cent of national income, is a different matter.) The prospective aid recipient may attempt to improve its international image by suitable window-dressing and statements of intent — but it will hardly alter its practice.

Donors are generally cautious about exercising such leverage too aggressively. Some will argue that to cut off all aid may result in total severance of relations and hence the loss of any chance of influencing policies. The major powers, competing for the favours of certain regimes, will hesitate to lose them because of an overriding concern for social justice. The most authoritarian regimes are often those most willing and able to play off one donor against another. French support of certain African countries and, at least until recently, American support to regimes in Central America, suggest that a concern for social justice is in many cases not a dominant feature in foreign policy.

Leverage is sometimes applied at sectoral level. The British government, for example, decided in 1975 to lay particular emphasis on rural development, with the stated aim of benefitting the poorest people in recipient countries. Many other countries which have also stressed the importance of 'aid to the poorest' have translated this into an emphasis on certain sectors, especially agriculture, or parts of sectors — primary schooling, rural water supplies etc.

Whether this works and whether it is in the interest of the people of the recipient country are two separate questions. The limitation of the approach is that the leverage is not applied with sufficient precision. It is not enough to concentrate on the Ministry of Agriculture rather than the Ministry of Transport, for example, in order to help the rural poor. The former might spend the funds on an uneconomic state farm, while the latter could provide feeder roads in rural areas. If leverage is to be exerted for the sake of the poorest it can be effective only if applied with precision — probably at project level. In so far as it is exerted at sectoral level it certainly has the effect of changing the pattern of sectoral investment; it is far more doubtful, however, whether this results in significant benefit to the poorer sections of the community.

Leverage is also applied at the project level. Donors will both propose specific types of project, and reject requests made to them, in the interest of social justice. In the field of housing, for example, it is common for donors to express interest in financing a 'site and service' scheme (whereby beneficiaries are provided not with a house, but simply a serviced site and financial assistance) even though the recipient country has no plans to undertake such a project, and may even oppose the idea.

Rejecting aid requests, as opposed to making proposals, can be rather difficult, once matters go beyond the initial stages; but this does nevertheless happen. Thus, a bilateral donor with particular concern for social justice was requested to finance an urban land reclamation scheme in Asia. The visiting appraisal mission was doubtful whether the project would actually benefit the poorest — in fact it seemed uncomfortably like a typical prestige project. Nevertheless, a full appraisal had to be carried out, and the mission could not commit themselves to a view, having to wait for the out-come of the report to their agency. Eventually the scheme was indeed turned down, and it was fairly clear, both from the nature of the response and the questions put by the appraisal mission, that the project request was refused on the grounds that the benefits would not accrue to those most in need.

The effectiveness of this kind of policy is reduced if a second donor is willing to replace the agency that refuses the project. Of course, it is true that time is wasted while the first donor is appraising it, since the second agency is not likely to consider it at the same time. This offers another strategy to a donor which is ardently opposed to a project. A member of a major bilateral agency in South America once assured me that they had agreed to appraise the feasibility of a new prestige airport project, which they firmly believed to be non-viable, in order to try and dis-courage and delay its eventual financing.

Donors may, of course, take up a coordinated stance. There are now several 'aid consortia' and other formal arrangements for discussions between donors, and most missions will have meetings with other agencies in the country concerned and inevitably will hear, and be influenced by, their views — whether these are well-justified opinions or mere prejudices.

Even if a donor cannot be found for a project, the prospective recipient may be able to achieve the same end by 'switching'. In other words, the finance provided by the donor for another priority project may allow local funds to be made available for the project turned down by the donor, thus cancelling out the intended effect of the leverage. This possibility lends support to the view that positive rather than negative discrimination is more effective i.e. a donor who wishes to influence policy in this direction (or indeed in other directions) should actively support projects which may not even be in the Development Plan at all, thus avoiding the possibility of switching.

With the above reservations, it appears that this type of leverage is effective. It works best, however, only if it is explicit. It is no use discriminating against a particular project on the grounds that it has a regressive effect on income distribution unless this reason is made clear to the frustrated recipient. Otherwise the educational effect will be lost. It is, unfortunately, unrealistic to expect that the superiority of the type of project favoured by the donor will be so evident in the long run that the recipient country will come to see the errors of its ways by example rather than by persuasion. An explicit policy of discrimination on grounds of a concern for social justice will inevitably have some effect. Unfortunately its effect will be least precisely in those countries where it is most needed.

The way a project is carried out is also subject to leverage. Just as it may be necessary to discriminate between projects rather than simply sectors to ensure social justice, so it may well also be necessary to discriminate between different ways of implementing a favoured project. The beneficiaries can vary widely according to the way in which the project is designed and implemented.

For example, a water supply project might appear to be one which would benefit the poorer groups, but the design and tariff system are of crucial importance. If water is supplied mainly through subsidised private connections, with few if any public standposts, the only beneficiaries will be those who are rich enough to have a house which is recognised as a legal structure, and therefore have a right to a private connection.

The example quoted above of the 'site and service' housing scheme is also not as simple as it might appear. Even with this approach, which is far preferable to the construction of a few high-cost units, the World Bank has found there is a tendency for 'upward drift' of the beneficiaries. A 'target group' is identified of those who are intended to benefit from the scheme (generally not by name, but by income group). But as the project progresses, design modifications are introduced, often as a result of pressure from politicians or local health officers, costs escalate in real terms, and it is found that if the repayment terms are tied to the actual final costs, the people that can afford the plots are not the poorest groups. To avoid such situations the donor agency becomes even more closely involved in the detailed planning and implementation of their projects.

Leverage is therefore also exerted at this level, to try and ensure that the donor agency's intention to help the poorest is not diverted

or distorted. The effect is obviously to interfere considerably in
the decision-making processes of the government. The precise way
in which this happens depends on the organisation of the project.
The donor agency may implement as well as plan it, and gain almost
a free hand in the way it operates the scheme itself. On small
projects, particularly those financed by charitable organisations,
this is quite common. On larger projects, and those where the
recipient government provides most of the project staff, leverage
has to be applied more indirectly — by influencing decisions at
meetings, writing appraisal reports, etc. Although the effect is
almost certainly to benefit the poorer groups, the good intentions
of the donor agency are somewhat offset by their ignorance of
local conditions, and against the advantages of this type of leverage
must be set the cost in terms of additional time and effort expended,
and the antagonism aroused in the recipient government by the
donor's interference.

Efficiency and Good Management

I now turn to the third type of leverage — that which is exerted in
order to foster efficiency and good management on the part of the
recipient country. This is most strongly associated with the
activities of the IMF. Although this is not a source of aid in the
strict sense of the term, its policies and activities are linked with
those of multilateral and bilateral aid agencies, and the effects of
its leverage are the subject of continuing, and often angry, debate.
   President Nyerere of Tanzania has stated, with engaging
simplicity, the predicament which some recipient countries find
themselves in:

> The poor Minister of Finance goes to the International Monetary
> Fund for assistance. He needs money and the fund requires him
> to fulfil certain conditions. He is worried because I talk about
> ideals all the time. I ask him to reject the conditions. 'But
> President, how will I fill the *gap*?' I realise I have to acquiesce
> because I have an objective to achieve. I promise myself next
> time I will be tougher.[3]

Some of the accusations made against the IMF have not been wholly proven: that the policies which it requires countries to follow are always the same, despite the wide variety of different problems and contexts; that they are concerned solely with growth and not with the distribution of its benefits, and so on. What is not in dispute, however, is that IMF assistance is conditional, and tied to the acceptance of certain measures specified by the fund such as removal of subsidies, increases in interest rates, and reduction in public spending. What is also beyond dispute, although not often openly stated, is that bilateral and multilateral agencies take considerable note of the IMF's relations with prospective recipient countries. The support of the fund is taken both as some indication of the country's financial viability, and an assurance that its policies will be monitored and to some extent kept in line by the wise men of the IMF.

Perhaps in part because of this, other bilateral and multilateral aid agencies do not themselves generally apply leverage at country level. It is true that in their search for viable projects, and in their desire to ensure that funds are actually spent, they will be drawn towards countries which are efficient — at least in terms of getting things done. But this is not the result of a policy to encourage efficiency by this means, and cannot be regarded as leverage.

A similar argument applies at sectoral level. Donors will favour regions or sectors which demonstrate an ability to absorb funds. Transport, for example, is an attractive sector because a new road, using foreign consultants and contractors, can be built with little reliance being placed on the local Ministry of Transport. The agriculture sector, on the other hand, tends to suffer because of the difficulty of ensuring that funds are spent according to schedule.

This, however, is not leverage in the strict sense of the term, since whatever its effect may be its intention is not to alter the sectoral balance. But sectoral leverage is sometimes exerted by aid donors who believe, not in their own interest or that of social justice, but simply in order to avoid wastage and inefficiency, that certain sectors need to be concentrated upon by the recipient country. Such views are pressed not only by providing or withholding aid, but also through advice either by visiting missions

and aid agency representatives, or by resident advisers and consultants to government. This means of exerting influence requires
some elaboration, and is dealt with at greater length below. Here I
am concerned only with the case in which such advice is backed
up by the promise of additional aid, or the threat of aid withheld.

This is most common where the donor is a major source of aid
and hence rather closely involved in the country's policies —
typically the former colonial power. France and Britain in
African countries are the obvious examples. The actual effect of
such leverage appears to vary. Thus the ODI studies of British aid
in Africa found that although ODM attempted to affect the
sectoral balance of investments its influence was only very limited
in Southern Africa, although quite considerable in Kenya.[4]

The way in which projects are carried out is also the subject of
leverage, in order to try and maximise the overall benefit of the
scheme. Thus a donor may not only express concern with the
details of the project at the planning stage, but also maintain a
continuing interest in its implementation. This may involve visiting
missions, or a permanent presence, perhaps in the form of advisers
provided under technical assistance with the project. The degree of
intervention depends very much upon the donor. Some may
virtually disappear once the funds have been handed over. Often,
however, the project will be divided into two or more stages and
further financing will be dependent on the satisfactory completion
of each, or there may be quarterly or annual disbursements of
funds subject to the donor's satisfaction with the way in which the
project is being carried out.

Certainly this approach is effective, especially if continued
during implementation as well as at the planning stage. Obviously
there is room for negotiation and compromise, but a donor with
the power to withhold funds from a project which is under way
does wield considerable influence if he chooses to use it. In such
circumstances the effect of leverage is to bring about the result
desired by the donor. Whether or not this actually leads to greater
efficiency depends on the extent of the donor's understanding of
the problem.

Finally, control is also sometimes exercised on the rate at
which projects are implemented. Thus the World Bank, for example,

may draw up a detailed schedule of targets to be met and decisions to be taken by specified dates, perhaps at monthly intervals. Failure to meet these deadlines can result in mild rebuke or heavy threats of withholding further disbursements. This may seem paradoxical – recipients are told, in effect, that if they fail to spend their money faster they will not be given any more – but it certainly acts as a stimulus, albeit a rather aggravating one.

The question which I have not yet resolved is whether this third type of leverage should properly be classified under category one, or two, or neither. The answer depends on whether the concept of 'efficiency and good management' is regarded as free of ideological content. To take one extreme, the IMF may require a country to cut subsidies on consumption goods because it believes this to be the right way to run the economy. A bilateral donor might even try to do the same, if it was a sufficiently important source of finance. Although the donor would claim it was acting in the interest of the people of the recipient country (as well as protecting its own funds, in the case of a loan) others would regard it as neo-imperialism by capitalist powers, and an attempt to impose a free enterprise ideology. At the other extreme, the donor agency may exert leverage in connection with very practical and technical issues. The improved design of roads, more time-saving accounting procedures, less wasteful stockholding practices – these are issues where the concept of efficiency is relatively value-free.

Between these two extremes lies a whole range of issues which are more difficult to categorise. A donor agency, for example, may state as a condition of a loan, or even a grant, for a water supply project, that the tariff levels be set at a certain level. While this may be efficient in that it ensures the financial viability of the authority concerned, it also represents a distortion of government policies and will have an effect (either regressive or progressive) on the distribution of income.

The proponents of free enterprise would probably choose to classify this type of leverage under category two, while their opponents would try to distinguish the different varieties and categorise some under category one and others under category two. In view of the special nature of this type of leverage, and the lack of any objective measure of classification, I prefer to keep it as a third and separate category.

Terms of Aid

In addition to providing or withholding aid, there is another choice open to donors. They may vary the terms on which aid is given. Thus the rate of interest, the length of the grace period during which interest and repayments are suspended, and the repayment period of the loan can all be varied. This is not strictly another 'level' at which leverage can be applied, but rather a mechanism which allows 'fine tuning', a means by which the choice between providing or withholding aid can be less crudely applied.

In practice, although this possibility does exist, the terms of aid are generally not varied in this way, but are determined by other considerations. In general, grants and soft loans are provided only to the poorest countries. There is a cut-off point expressed in terms of *per capita* income which determines, for example, whether a country is eligible for an IDA credit (on soft terms) or a World Bank loan (on rather harder terms). Several other agencies operate a similar system. In addition, however, the terms of aid may vary according to the sector — whether it is 'productive' or 'non-productive'. The World Bank takes the view that loans to the former should be on hard terms, even to a poor country, in order to stimulate good management and ensure that projects are financially viable. The apparent contradiction between this policy and the desire to lend on soft terms to poor countries is resolved by lending on easy terms to the recipient government which then lends on to the appropriate agency in the country (e.g. the electricity board) on terms which are more nearly commercial.

In summary, therefore, although the terms of aid could be varied so as to allow a more precise form of leverage to be applied — whether to distinguish between countries, sectors or projects — this is not generally done.

Multilateral and Bilateral Donors

The discussion in previous sections highlights the importance of differentiating between types of donor — especially between multi-laterals and bilaterals. I have not so far made this distinction, in order to avoid complicating the analysis even further. But it is necessary now to correct this shortcoming.

I shall differentiate between four types of donor agency. The first is the bilaterals, that is individual donor countries. The second is the United Nations specialised agencies such as the World Health Organisation, UNICEF, FAO, etc. The third is the regional banks such as Asian and Inter-American Development Banks. The fourth is the World Bank. I shall not refer specifically to other agencies which are not covered by the above typology e.g. the voluntary agencies, the European Development Fund or the OPEC funds.

I do not propose to discuss in detail the differences between all these agencies, but only to concentrate on four aspects which tend to determine the extent and method of leverage which each type of agency is likely to apply. The four aspects are their attitudes to self-interest, social justice, and good management (the three motives for leverage identified above) and the extent to which each type of agency is controlled by the developing countries — obviously a further factor of significance in this context. Clearly I shall be making some rather dangerous generalisations, to which numerous exceptions can no doubt be found. Nevertheless it is possible to distinguish between the different types of agency in these ways, and the validity of the conclusions which logically follow are largely borne out by the empirical evidence.

Self-interest as a factor is clearly of more importance to bilaterals than to the three types of multilateral distinguished. Beyond this it is worth mentioning only two points. First, the UN specialised agencies do, in a sense, have self-interest to consider. Each has a mandate which confines its activities in certain respects and charges it with specific aims. UNICEF, for example, must justify its activities in terms of how they benefit children. To apply such a policy would not usually be described as leverage. On the other hand there can be no doubt that UNICEF is more likely to favour projects, sectors and maybe even countries in which the interests of children are predominant. This concern also extends to UNICEF's actively seeking to ensure that the method of implementation of projects is such as to maximise the benefits to children. In this sense, therefore, it is true to say that aid is here used to 'ensure compliance of the recipient with some form of action desired by the donor' and therefore leverage, according to my definition of the term, is being applied.

The second point I wish to make is that regional banks also have a mandate which, *inter alia*, is to encourage the integrated development of the region as a whole. In practice the extent to which this aim determines their selection of countries, sectors and projects is rather limited. It cannot, however, be totally ignored. In so far as such considerations are important (and I would argue that this is less than the extent to which, for example, UNICEF's activities are determined by the interests of children) it may be accurately stated that, according to my definition of the term, these agencies are exerting leverage.

The second factor under consideration is the furtherance of social justice. Here again it is the bilaterals (or some of them) which are most likely to exert leverage. I am not here suggesting that multilaterals have a total disregard for social justice, but I am claiming that they are less likely to exert leverage to try and ensure that it is brought about.

The third factor is efficiency and good management. Here, I would argue, the order is reversed. It is the banks which have the greatest concern for good management, and are most prepared to exert leverage to seek to ensure that it is achieved. Some would claim that they have a mandate to do so. The UN specialised agencies and the bilaterals are less likely to choose countries, sectors or projects on the basis of whether they will encourage good management, and are less likely to attempt to exercise control over the method and rate of implementation of projects, for the purposes of improving efficiency.

The fourth factor I consider is the extent to which donor agencies are controlled by developing countries. Bilateral agencies, of course, are not so controlled. The World Bank, despite being an international body, is much less subject to control than the specialised agencies of the UN. The regional banks are, to varying extents, controlled by the developing countries in the region which they cover. The Asian Development Bank, at one extreme, is largely dominated by the USA and Japan. The African Development Bank, by contrast, is controlled by the African countries. The Inter-American Development Bank, despite having the USA as a major contributor, is, for a number of reasons, mainly controlled by the Latin American countries themselves.

This fourth factor has significance, of course, for all the others. It is partly because they are answerable to the developing countries that multilaterals are less likely than bilateral donors to discriminate between countries (and to a lesser extent sectors) on the basis of any consideration — whether it be self-interest, the furtherance of social justice, or of good management. The last of these considerations, however, the furtherance of good management, involves not so much discrimination between countries and sectors as concern for the details of implementation. (Here I exclude the IMF as not being a source of 'official development assistance'.) A very general conclusion can therefore be drawn from this brief analysis, that in terms of the way in which they exert leverage the bilaterals discriminate more between countries, while the multilaterals exert a greater influence in the day-to-day implementation of projects.

The Role of Technical Assistance

A large proportion of foreign aid is provided in the form of technical assistance. It accounts for half of French aid, for example, and 20 per cent of total aid from OECD countries. Some of the advisers and consultants financed by these funds will work on the preparation and appraisal of projects, or their actual implementation. Others will be attached to the recipient governments — as teachers and nurses, perhaps, or as advisers in the Treasury or Ministry of Agriculture. In this section I am concerned with their possible role in the exercise of leverage.

This type of aid, like financial assistance, could be promised or withheld in order to influence the recipient's actions. In fact this

is very rarely done. (Again, I exclude military assistance.) The most
likely reason is that unless the personnel concerned are in operation-
al positions, the recipient country may not feel that their presence
or absence is of crucial importance.

Advisers and consultants can, of course, be agents of leverage
of the types already described. Thus, if the donor agency wishes to
exercise control over the method of implementation of a project
it can insist that it provide personnel to act as advisers, or even to
undertake the implementation of the project themselves. Also, a
donor agency may use consultants to produce reports from which
specific recommendations follow, and make the provision of
financial assistance conditional on the acceptance of these
recommendations. Thus, a multilateral agency finances a
water supply tariff study for a city and makes the proposed loan
conditional on the recipient government's agreement to the consultant's report.

This must be distinguished from the situation where influence
is exerted by individual advisers or consultants, but not by virtue
of their being linked directly to the provision or withholding of
aid. Such individuals can acquire considerable power and influence,
and their views can alter the decisions taken by the governments
concerned. Their influence, however, does not derive from any
direct or explicit connection between them and the promise of
financial assistance. Clearly, in the case of a major donor, the
recipient government will not wish to antagonise and oppose too
many of the advisers that are provided — but this is more in the
general interest of maintaining good relations with the donor.
Even in this situation, it cannot be assumed that the views of the
adviser are controlled by, or are even the same as, the policies of
the donor agency. Bilateral donors will naturally recruit personnel
who appear not only to have the necessary skills but also to hold
views which appear reasonable, and having posted them may keep
in touch with what they are doing. But such people are rarely on
the permanent staff of the agency, and would not consider themselves as subject to its direction with regard to the policies they
recommend. Advisers financed by multilateral agencies may have
more permanent connections, and their views would then tend
more closely to reflect those of their employer.

In summary, therefore, considerable influence is undoubtedly exercised through the provision of technical assistance, but this should not be classified as a type of leverage, nor should it be assumed that the personnel who exert such influence are necee necessarily subject to the control and direction of the agencies that finance them.

The Merits and Demerits of Leverage

I shall now address the question of whether or not leverage, in its many different forms, should be applied. I shall judge this in two respects: first, a purely subjective assessment of whether it is morally defensible; secondly, a more pragmatic question as to whether the exercise of leverage antagonises the recipient to an unacceptable extent.

I shall first consider the case where a donor's self-interest is the motive. If this type of leverage is applied at country level it is defensible only if the term 'aid' is abandoned altogether. If a country wishes to build a military base, or to avoid the nationalisation of its citizens' investments in a foreign country, then it is reasonable that it should offer the country concerned payment in exchange for such consideration. On the assumption that a bargain is reached freely and in full knowledge by both parties, such an arrangement is not morally reprehensible. To describe such a transaction as aid, however, is grossly misleading. The problem is that such payments are commonly included in the statistics of aid flows, and are often cited by the donor countries as evidence of their generosity. This is regrettable, not only because of its hypocrisy, but also because it damages the whole of the aid relationship.

As I have suggested above, leverage for the purpose of self-interest may be applied at sector or project level if the donor hopes thereby to please a specific individual or group. Such leverage is rarely, if ever, made explicit and may best be described as bribery.

The tying of aid, which is the means by which leverage is exerted at the project implementation level, is certainly not a practice that is in the interests of the developing world. The

Annual Review of the Development Assistance Committee of the OECD constantly stresses the need to do away with this practice, but bilateral agencies have been slow to respond.

The second motive to consider is the furtherance of social justice. Although I assume this is a desirable objective, some doubts do arise: first, the question whether such leverage should be explicit. One may argue that it is unfair on a country if it is not told that the reason it has not received aid, or the reason why one sector is not favoured, is because the donor is concerned principally with the furtherance of social justice. It may also be argued that it is self-defeating not to make such a policy explicit, since the thwarted recipient cannot amend his policies in the way intended unless he is aware of the criterion by which he has been discriminated against. There is, however, a counter-argument. If the donor is seeking to change the recipient's policies by example rather than by persuasion then the need to make its policy explicit is removed. Unfortunately this is unrealistic. It would require that the projects chosen by the donor be not only better, but also seen to be better by the recipient country, which would therefore be persuaded, by example, to adopt the donor's policies. Although the argument is tenable, I do not believe that practice would lend it support. I therefore suggest that if leverage is applied by donors in the interests of social justice, this should be made explicit, and that there is nothing reprehensible in such a policy.

The degree of concern with social justice, and the stated commitment to liberal and even socialist policies among bilateral aid donors, is sometimes remarkable in comparison with the domestic and foreign policies of their own governments. Land reform measures, progressive tariff systems etc. which are eagerly thrust on recipient countries would often be unacceptable if suggested at home – a point which does not escape the recipient agencies.

The case for applying leverage in the interests of efficiency and good management has already been discussed. Clearly the conclusion depends on one's ideological bias. Where the issues are purely technical in nature it is beneficial to exert leverage (assuming, of course, that the donor agency has greater technical competence than the recipient). Where ideological issues begin to enter, it is not. In general, with regard to leverage applied at all levels, unless there is clear congruence between the ideology of the donor and recipient country, the onus should be on the donor to ensure that its actions do not distort the stated policies of the recipient.

I turn now to the question of whether the exercise of leverage antagonises recipients. The short answer is that it always does — but to very varying degrees. Before going into detail, let me make two general points. First, if leverage does not work it should not be used. Obviously, if nothing is achieved by it, the best policy is not to risk antagonism by trying. Secondly, the extent of antagonism caused by withholding aid is greater, the more expectations have been raised that it will be provided. If there are specific conditions associated with the provision of aid, and these are made clear early in the negotiations, the degree of antagonism which they provoke is likely to be minimised.

The parties that might be antagonised by the exercise of leverage are, broadly, politicians, civil servants and the public. In many cases, however, most of these will be unaware of the situation. The details of aid negotiations are generally not widely known or discussed outside the ministry and location concerned. The public at large, and many politicians and civil servants, are therefore unaware of anything beyond the fact that aid has been granted by a particular country for a particular purpose. If leverage has been applied they are unaware of it.

Within the ministry or location affected there will certainly be concern. This is most keenly felt not in the discrimination between sectors and projects, but with regard to control over the method and rate of implementation of projects. Neither ministers nor civil servants like to feel that they are being constrained or criticised by the donor agency. A minister does not enjoy having to change his policies in order to satisfy a donor, and a civil servant does not enjoy having to submit monthly reports on how many miles of road have been built, or whether agreement has been reached on the acquisition of land.

Although exerting leverage will always tend to antagonise people, the extent to which this occurs is least when such leverage is exerted at the level of the sector or the project. A minister or civil servant will be disappointed if his sector is not chosen, but will feel no particular antagonism towards the donor agency concerned provided it has not first raised his expectations.

Leverage applied at country level will be evident only to the very few ministers and senior civil servants concerned, unless they choose to publicise it; but the antagonism aroused can, in this case, be very intense. By contrast, the antagonism aroused by interference in the details of planning and implementation may be more widespread, since it affects the civil servants with whom the donor agencies are probably dealing on a day-to-day basis; but the intensity of this antagonism is likely to be less.

Conclusion

It is clear from the foregoing that it is important to distinguish many different types of leverage. They are not all to the detriment of the prospective recipients; nor is leverage invariably applied. In many cases the recipient country's wishes are granted without significant modification, and the implementation of the programme project is effected without interference by the donor. But even in such cases the whole complex process of aid has to be gone through, with the consequential delays and distortions. Thus, the exercise of leverage not only creates problems directly, but also indirectly by necessitating the perpetuation of a machinery which is ill-adapted to its stated purpose of allowing aid to flow efficiently to those in need.

Notes

1. *Partners in Development*, Report of the Commission on International Development (Pall Mall Press, London, 1969).

2. Mahbub ul Haq, 'Tied Credits — A Quantitative Analysis' in J.H. Adler (ed.), *Capital Movements and Economic Development* (Macmillan, London, 1967).

3. Julius Nyerere, 'Third World Negotiating Strategy', *Third World Quarterly*, vol. I, no. 2 (April, 1977).

4. Rob Wood and Kathryn Morton, 'Has British Aid Helped Poor Countries? — Five African Cases', *ODI Review*, no. I (1977).

4 MOTIVES AND INTERESTS

I turn now to the motives and interests of those involved in the giving and receiving of aid, in order to identify the further distortions that these can cause in addition to those attributable to the machinery of aid. Official statements of why countries give aid are often confusing and contradictory. Thus, while governments assert that concern for the people of the Third World is a major consideration, they also stress the importance of supporting friendly nations, of saving countries from communism (or capitalism), encouraging the spread of a free market (or socialist) ideology, protecting raw material sources, stimulating exports, etc. Fortunately my concern is not with the stated policies and motives of governments but with the interests of specific parties within the aid process. Nevertheless it is worthwhile to note in passing that the confused objectives just referred to are to some extent reflected in the confusion amongst the administrators of aid who are required to put the policies into practice.

I shall distinguish five different parties in the aid process: the politicians and civil servants on the donor side, their counterparts on the recipient side, and the intermediaries — the contractors, consultants and advisers. For each group I shall discuss what is their interest in aid, and what, if anything, is the effect of this on the nature of the aid process.

Politicians on the Donor Side

Politicians from donor countries are generally not particularly interested in foreign aid. In this respect they reflect the opinion of the majority of people, who are neither well informed nor particularly favourably inclined towards it. Since it is also, in economic terms, rather inconsequential it is not surprising that as a vote-catching activity it has little appeal. To quote John White:

> Public opinion is most significant as a determinant of governmental action or inaction in those areas of policy by which the public at large is most significantly affected. Minor expenditures on activities in far-off places is not one such area.[1]

In the USA support for foreign aid grew at a time when it was seen as playing a significant part in the Cold War. The current decline in interest in the USA may be traced partly to disenchantment with policies in Latin America and South East Asia, but also, as in other Western countries, to the economic recession. But in some other countries such as Scandinavia and the Netherlands, aid appears to enjoy more popular support and the volume has been growing.

The minister responsible for foreign aid will, of course, seek to maximise the budget allocated, especially if he or she has a particular interest in the subject. Other ministries however, will not only compete for funds but may also wish to change the way in which aid is used. Yet even this constraint is of limited significance. To quote from Judith Hart:

> The functions and responsibilities of overseas aid and development are unlikely in the future to impinge greatly upon most home departments. Nor does it have a basis of electoral popularity. It follows that its strengths and weaknesses will be largely determined by its minister.[2]

It is difficult to establish the importance of special interest groups and their power to influence the amount and direction of aid, but a study was carried out on behalf of the Pearson Commission which concluded that in Britain at least their significance was small. To quote John White: ' . . . no unofficial entity constituted an effective source of pressure on the central policy decisions concerning the developmental content of the British aid programme in the late 1960s, with the possible exception of new overseas investors.'[3]

There have, of course, been individual cases of politicians with specific interests in a certain project or country, or representing the interests of another party, who have sought to influence particular decisions, but there appears to be no effective pressure group operating so as to modify the pattern of aid in Britain. One is tempted to wonder who decides on aid policy, and why they decide as they do. Politicians certainly play a relatively minor part.

Civil Servants on the Donor Side

In this category I include all those employed by aid agencies, whether bilateral or multilateral. They are concerned largely with their career prospects and job satisfaction, and the success of their own agency. They may have a specific interest in development and concern for the people of the Third World, but this is by no means invariable. Their major concern therefore is to do what their agency requires. In simple terms what this means is that, having been told the size of their budget, they must ensure that as much of it gets spent as possible (subject, of course, to the even stronger imperative of avoiding over-expenditure). These two aims result in a desire to maximise their own flexibility in adjusting the rate of expenditure so as to steer a passage between the Scylla of underspending and the Charybdis of excess.

Next they want to ensure that the funds are spent on good projects. Such projects must be consistent with the objectives of the donor country and, as far as is compatible with this, yield benefits to the people of the recipient country concerned. But what are the objectives of the donor country? By reading official statements on the subject one obtains an extremely confused picture. This is for two reasons: first that there is indeed some real confusion in the minds of those who state the policy, as to why aid is given at all, and secondly there is a need to persuade two very different audiences — both the electorate of the donor country and the international community — that such aid is a good thing.

Some bilateral agencies claim only that their aid is in the interest of the poor recipients. Others tend to attach more weight to donor interests. The British government's line in 1975 appeared to compromise:

> Moreover, while the criterion used in H.M.G's aid policy is
> primarily that of need, the allocation of U.K. aid, like that of
> other donors, is conditioned by a number of considerations
> reflecting our wider interests and historical links. These will
> include political and commercial factors.[4]

Under the new Conservative government the line shifted even
further. The British government introduced 'new arrangements . . .
to ensure a greater degree of commercial orientation in so far as is
compatible with UK aid policy.'[5]

In the United States, at the beginning of the 1970s, the Peterson
Report, although in favour of increasing aid, recommended 'to
establish a framework of principles, procedures and institutions
that will assure the effective use of assistance funds *and the achieve-
ment of US national interests*' (my italics).[6] The current United
States policy, like that of Britain, would place still more emphasis
on donor interest.

United Nations publications, seeking to explain and gain support
for what the United Nations does, lay stress not only on the benefits
to the aid recipients but also on the (sometimes disproportionate)
benefits to the donors.

> Another factor to keep in mind is that several of the major
> donors to the United Nations system get their money back
> because the United Nations spends most of it in developed
> countries. Geographically, 41 per cent of the United Nations
> regular budget is spent in New York, 30 per cent at Geneva, 11
> per cent at Vienna and the balance at about 60 duty stations
> around the world. . . . UNDP estimates that it puts back into
> the United States economy, mainly through salaries of experts
> and purchases of equipment, 35 per cent more dollars than it
> gets from the United States contribution.[7]

Because of the need to satisfy different audiences the official
statements of policy probably represent fairly accurately the real
mix of conflicting objectives. But they do not provide their civil

servants with very clear or useful guidelines as to how they are to act.

An important consideration, not often explicitly stated, is the need to avoid antagonising any important group, whether in the donor or recipient country. A specific example will elucidate the point. A major bilateral agency was assessing its aid policy to a Middle Eastern country. It had given considerable support to an irrigation scheme and was now considering involvement in the urban sector. Despite the fact that the former scheme had been largely unsuccessful because of inadequate project design, there was strong support for a similar one, in contrast to the proposed urban involvement, because of the fear that the latter was more risky in political terms, and that any failure would be more stark. Risk aversion is certainly a factor of considerable importance in guiding the decisions of donor civil servants, but the types of risk feared are not necessarily those that will redound to the cost of the recipient.

In summary, the donor civil servant is typically cautious but well intentioned, owing allegiance to masters who give rather unclear guidance as to what is expected. Their power is, perhaps, more than they realise. Aid is given by individuals and committees representing the people of the donor country. The day-to-day decisions of these individuals and committees are what, in the final analysis, determine aid policies. This point is made strongly by John White who, in his book *The Politics of Foreign Aid* set out to answer the question I raised at the end of the previous section: who makes aid policy? His conclusion was, to quote his final sentence, that 'The makings of aid policy lie in the hands of those who actually administer it.'[8] But these administrators, lacking clear direction, and intent on satisfying the requirements of their agency, tend to attach considerable importance to minimising risk and minimising commitments, aims which are not necessarily in the best interests of the prospective recipients of aid.

Politicians on the Recipient Side

By contrast with those in donor countries the politicians in the

receiving countries have a strong and easily explainable interest in
aid. It is the ministers who are most concerned. They may well
regard aid as in the wider national interest, provided it is on good
terms and with minimum strings attached. But it is certainly considered to be in the ministry's, and hence the minister's interest, to
receive as much aid as possible, provided it is not accompanied by
leverage which unduly constrains the minister's freedom of
decision.

All politicians, including ministers, will also have an interest in
aid in so far as it affects or may affect their constituents, or
certain specific sectors or groups, such as the business community
or the farmers. They may also have a direct material interest.
These considerations may be or relevance to the location of the
project, to the type of project, or to some other aspect of its
design.

Such self-interested concerns by those in power have led to
some of the more stark failures in development aid. A steel works
may be located far from both deep water and iron ore deposits, but
within the electorate of the minister concerned. The choice of
which port to expand, where to build a university, what land to
acquire for development — all these and more may be crucially
affected by the nature of constituency boundaries or the pattern of
land ownership. Clearly aid donors are not unaware of such facts,
but they may find it hard to resist the pressure. The representatives
of donor agencies have to find projects on which to spend their
funds, and in doing so they cannot afford to antagonise powerful
ministers, and will be reluctant to risk doing so. The general lack
of data and the impossibility of choosing on a totally scientific
and objective basis, the right site for a certain development, or of
the appropriate priority ranking of a number of water supplies, make
it only too easy to compromise, and to convince oneself that any
project is better than none.

Despite the many examples of aid projects that have suffered in
this way, the subject is, understandably perhaps, not well documented. Kathryn Morton, however, in her book about aid to
Malawi, describes a situation which exemplifies the point I am
making. 'Efforts were made to improve project appraisal methods
— although these were largely irrelevant to the choice of certain

major projects included because of Dr Banda's unswerving and virtually unchallengeable conviction that they were needed.'[9]

An additional factor of importance is the preponderant concern of politicians to show the electorate that they have 'delivered the goods'. As well as affecting the sector or location favoured, this also leads to an inordinate concern for projects which are highly visible and which yield rapid results. Such projects are all too often not in the best interest of development. Examples may be quoted of water towers being built although no water has been found to fill them, or of factories ceremonially opened although the raw materials are not available to supply them. With an eye on the next election politicians must make the best of the opportunities that arise, and aid may present such an opportunity.

Civil Servants on the Recipient Side

I turn now to the civil servants in the recipient country. Their main interest, like their counterparts in the donor country, is to satisfy their agency and hence ensure their career prospects. In certain cases they may, as with their politicians, have a personal material interest — as a landowner perhaps. (In a recent planning study in the Middle East the bilateral funding agency was surprised to find the amount of land scheduled for development which was owned by members of the planning staff.)

The generally held view in developing countries is that aid is a 'good thing'. Various economic theories have identified different 'gaps' that have to be filled if growth is to be achieved: an investment gap, a foreign exchange gap, a lack of skilled manpower. Whichever theory is favoured, it is widely believed in developing countries that foreign aid can usefully contribute to filling one or more of these gaps. (Generally, it is the need for foreign exchange that is the most compelling.) There have certainly been countries which have found the strings attached to such aid unacceptable, and there is a body of opinion which rejects the acceptance of aid whatever the terms, either on principle or on the basis of its manifest failings. In general, however, civil servants in recipient countries share the view that they need assistance and that, provided it can be obtained at reasonable cost, it should be accepted.

What is regarded as being 'reasonable cost' may differ between the Treasury and the line ministries. The civil servant from a line ministry will typically seek to maximise the amount of aid to his ministry, being concerned with the terms of aid not so much as they relate to rates of interest payable or repayment periods, but rather as to whether they restrict the ministry's freedom of action. The Treasury civil servant deals with the economy as a whole, and therefore tends to pay more attention to the relative attractiveness of the terms and the priority of the sector concerned.

There are other factors of importance to be considered. By associating with a foreign aid project, a civil servant may enjoy improved conditions – access to project vehicles, for example, or air-conditioning in the office, possibly more financial benefits, the chance of foreign travel and career advancement, and a certain amount of prestige. There is therefore an added incentive for any but the most xenophobic of civil servants to favour the acceptance of foreign aid. Such considerations may apply with less force to the most senior civil servants. To them, the advisers and experts the accompany aid may seem meddling and time-consuming, but the advantages of their presence are still usually seen as out-weighing their costs.

The Intermediaries

I turn now to the other parties involved in aid: foreign contractors, consultants and advisers. Contractors are those employed by aid agencies to carry out construction or similar work. Consultants may be hired to undertake feasibility studies or give advice, em-bodied in written reports. Advisers generally stay for rather longer than consultants (two years contracts being typical), have a more open-ended responsibility, and work more closely with a govern-ment department within the recipient country. Clearly these dis-tinctions can become rather blurred, but they are nevertheless useful and generally applicable.

Contractors

I shall deal first, and briefly, with contractors. Apart from a possible liking for travel the contractor's main interest lies in the financial success of his firm. This need not conflict with the accomplishment of his tasks. Some contractors are efficient and some are inefficient – but they do not necessarily distort aid policy. The effects, beneficial or otherwise, of the works that they undertake, depend mainly on the initial decision to undertake them and the outline designs of the road, bridge, irrigation system or whatever, which, in most cases, are the responsibility of others.

There are, however, two exceptions to this general point. First, contractors, in their desire to make money, may influence aid decisions in such a way as to further their own interest e.g. by direct approaches to those responsible in the donor agency. Secondly, in so far as they have freedom of decision – for example with regard to the detailed design of a road, or the technology to be used – their self-interest may run counter to that of the prospective beneficiaries of the project. Thus, for example, in determining the precise alignment of a road, they are likely to be more concerned with cost minimisation than the disruption of those living on the land; or, in selecting the method of construction, they will tend to choose that which ensures their profit although this may not be in the interest of increasing the employment of the local population.

In general one may say that they act as the agents of the donor country, but seek to further their own interest within the limits that this implies. A good example is afforded by American grain exporters assigned the task by the USA of shipping food aid to India under the PL 480 arrangement, and to Honduras as disaster relief following hurricane 'Fifi'. It was discovered in the former case that grain was deliberately and systematically short-weighted by 3 per cent, while in the latter case the quality of grain was so bad that it had to be dumped into the sea. The exporters had in each case taken the opportunity that aid offered to considerably increase their profits. Such distortions exemplify what can occur when the responsibility for carrying out an aid project lies with a commercial enterprise whose primary concern is profit.

Foreign Consultants

Perhaps of greater significance are the foreign consultants who can be, and generally are, closely involved in the aid process itself. Before examining the interests of the consultant it may be useful to explore the question of how and why consultants are used.

Foreign consultants may be hired to undertake feasibility studies or give technical advice. I shall consider each in turn. As discussed in Chapter 2, the preparation and appraisal of proposed projects is often done by consultants, paid for by an aid agency. The cost of their services is met mainly by the aid agency, out of their funds earmarked for the country concerned. The prospective recipient is responsible only for certain local costs, provision of office space, etc. Although they are nominally answerable to the recipient country as well as the donor agency, so that their initial selection as consultants and their reports are subject to the approval of the recipient country, in practice they owe ultimate allegiance to the donor agency. In many cases there is no conflict, and they can serve both masters, but when such a situation arises it is the interest of the paymaster that generally prevails.

A typical feasibility study might be to prepare an outline design for a multi-purpose dam, and assess its economic feasibility. A team of engineers, soil scientists, economists and others, possibly from several collaborating firms, would be awarded the job, in competition with a number of other firms, on the basis of their proposal describing how they would carry out the study and which staff would be used. The engineers would work on the design and costing of the dam, downstream irrigation works, power lines etc., based on Terms of Reference provided by the financing agency. The agriculturalists would recommend suitable cropping patterns, estimate yields, etc., and the economists would assess the economic feasibility of the scheme in terms of the estimated costs and benefits and perhaps recommend appropriate charging systems for electricity and water. A management consultant might also study the organisational changes that would be needed to operate the proposed new system. Others such as anthropologists and environmental specialists might also be involved. In most feasibility studies there is thus a team of people from different disciplines: engineers, economists, financial analysts, transport planners etc. Their job is rather rigidly defined in the Terms of Reference of the study, which require them to advise as to whether the proposed project is feasible, and hence, by implication, whether it should be financed by foreign aid.

This may be contrasted with the second type of assignment for foreign consultants — that of giving technical advice. This may range from an assessment of the suitability of a proposed water supply intake, the fertility of soil intended for irrigation, or the design of a new berth, to the organisational structure of a new corporation, the setting up of a new court system or the preservation of historic sites. In these types of study, the team may be smaller and involve fewer disciplines, the issues may be rather more technical in nature and, most important, the consultants are not required to consider the question of feasibility i.e. the decision as to whether or not to undertake a proposed course of action.

The significance of the distinction between these two types of assignment becomes clearer when we consider the consultant's interest and how this affects the aid process. The consultant is interested in his job satisfaction and career prospects, and the success of the firm for which he works. He may also have an interest in the well-being of the people of the developing world. His own success and that of his firm are both best assured by satisfying the agency which finances his assignments. His major concern is therefore to write reports which are acceptable to the donor agency. Often this will not conflict either with the interest of the recipient country or his own job satisfaction, but a few cases will demonstrate the types of problem that may arise.

A firm of consultants hired to carry out a tariff study, for example, will frequently find itself at the centre of controversy. The financing agency will wish to ensure the viability of the water supply or electricity supply that it proposes to finance, while the recipient country wishes to keep tariffs down — possibly in order not to lose votes. The consultants are unlikely, in such circumstances, to favour the views of the recipient country, since it is the donor agency which pays the bills.

In a study of a road project in South East Asia the multilateral financing agency concerned hired consultants who calculated that the internal rate of return on the project was less than that required for the approval of the agency's board. The consultants were therefore hired again to recalculate the internal rate of return taking into account more 'secondary benefits'. (These are the less immediate benefits which accrue as a result of an improved transport link, and are notoriously difficult to measure with accuracy.) In effect the consultant was being asked simply to boost the rate of return to an acceptable level.

In the case of technical advice rather than feasibility studies conflicts of interest are rather different. In a feasibility study the prospective recipient almost invariably wants an affirmative answer at all costs and the prospective donor would prefer an affirmative answer, while the facts may often not support such a conclusion. In the case of technical advice there are, of course, always interested parties. In one South Asian country, for example, the question of where to site the intake of a new water supply was of great interest to the local Member of Parliament. A location further upstream would have allowed the new system to supply a town in his electorate (albeit at enormous expense). In Egypt, the question of soil quality proved to be a major political issue since it cast doubt on the feasibility of the Aswan Dam. The dam was built on the basis that there was plentiful land of soil quality sufficient for economically viable irrigation. When a semi-detailed soil survey called this into question this 'technical' matter became the subject of political controversy.

Studies undertaken by consultants will very frequently be politically sensitive. Indeed, if there was no likelihood of controversy their services would often not be required. But the dominant interest of the consultant is to satisfy the financing agency, and this is particularly important in the case of feasibility studies. Indeed the consultant may be said to embody the major contradictions with which this book is concerned. He is answerable to both the donor agency and the recipient agency, but not to the people of either donor or recipient country. He is placed in the centre of a web of confused and conflicting interests, yet his instructions make no explicit reference to these conflicts, although it is implicitly intended that he will resolve them. To outward appearances he is equally the servant of both donor and recipient agency, with every act requiring the approval of both parties, but in the event of disagreement it is the donor rather than the recipient who has the last word, a consideration that influences every decision that the consultant makes. The consultant, therefore, although an important party in the aid process, tends mainly to reinforce the interest of the donor agency.

Advisers

The request for an adviser generally has to come from the prospective recipient — although it is quite common for such requests to be 'ventriloquised' by eager aid donors. In some cases the acceptance of advisers is one of the conditions attached to the provision of a loan. Thus the World Bank, for example, may specify that the accounting operations of an organisation to which they are lending money must be strengthened in this way.

Advisers, like consultants, wish to improve their career prospects, and are recruited and paid by the donor agency, although their appointment is subject to acceptance by the recipient country. In this respect they owe allegiance in just the same way as do consultants, but the difference is that their actions often do not impinge in any way upon the activities of the donor. While a consultant provides advice which may be acted upon by the donor agency, the adviser deals almost exclusively with the recipient country. Although the adviser is paid by the donor agency, this will in many cases have little effect on the way he does his job, even supposing that he feels a debt of allegiance.

He will, however, wish to satisfy the institution to which he is attached in the recipient country. He may be able to establish a good working relationship and contribute useful advice; or, on the other hand, be ignored — either because he was not really wanted in the first place, or because his views are not acceptable. In such circumstances the recipient country is very unlikely to complain to the donor agency. The cost to the recipient country is regarded as small, and they have no wish to antagonise a potential source of further aid; the only circumstances in which they are likely to object is if the adviser becomes too outspoken in his criticisms.

The adviser therefore has a strong incentive to keep a low profile, for although his job satisfaction may thus be reduced, there are pecuniary compensations. If he chooses to interfere and try to change policies he will arouse antagonism. But unless he does so, the aid agency that finances him will probably hear no complaints from the recipient country. In summary, therefore, unless they act as the agents of leverage (discussed in the last chapter) advisers are unlikely to cause distortions in the aid process, and their interests are best served by keeping a low profile.

Conclusion

It is clear from the foregoing that the different parties involved in the aid process are influenced by interests which are, on occasion, conflicting. It is the parties on the donor side that hold the ultimate power, but because of the unclear and largely inconsistent motives for giving aid, and the relative ignorance and lack of interest of politicians and special interest groups, the civil servants enjoy considerable powers. The politicians in the recipient country and, to a lesser extent the civil servants, can exercise a certain amount of control by virtue of their power to frustrate the attempts of donor civil servants to spend their aid budgets. The other parties involved — contractors, consultants and advisers — act, in the final analysis, as agents of the donors, but because of the freedom of action which the situation allows them they can, in certain circumstances, also play an important part in the aid process. In so far as their own individual interests differ from those of donor or of recipient this creates a further distorting factor.

Notes

1. John White, *The Politics of Foreign Aid* (The Bodley Head, London, 1974).
2. Judith Hart, *Aid and Liberation* (Victor Gollancz, London, 1973).

3. White, *The Politics of Foreign Aid*.

4. *The Changing Emphasis in British Aid Policies. More Help for the Poorest*, Cmnd 6270 (HMSO, London, 1975).

5. *Trade and Aid*, Cmnd 7213 (HMSO, London, 1978).

6. *US Foreign Assistance in the 1970s: a New Approach*, Report to the President from the Task Force on International Development. Quoted in George Cunningham, *The Management of Aid Agencies* (Croom Helm, London, 1974).

7. United Nations, *Image and Reality* (UN Dept. of Public Information, 1979).

8. White, *Politics of Foreign Aid*.

9. Kathryn Morton, *Aid and Dependence* (Croom Helm, London, 1975).

5 THE PROBLEMS OF FOREIGN AID

In this chapter I shall identify and analyse the practical problems of foreign aid, and the extent to which they are caused or exacerbated by the nature of the aid process. Because this is my specific concern, I will not include discussion of certain important criticisms of foreign aid, such as the fact that it may result, intentionally or otherwise, in the support of reactionary regimes, or that it leads to an increase in the foreign indebtedness of the recipient countries (at least in the case of loans). These issues are not unimportant, indeed they are rightly dealt with at length in other publications, but my concern is to focus attention specifically on those problems which are associated with the day-to-day mechanics of aid.

My purpose is not simply to be critical and destructive, but rather to demonstrate the complexity of the problems faced, and the extent to which they interrelate. I suggest that they are largely attributable not to incompetence or corruption but to the machinery of aid, the 'rules of the game', which have been devised by donors in such a way as to allow them to continue to exercise leverage — whether in their own self-interest or what they believe to be the interest of the prospective recipient. The administrators of aid are thus confronted by a very real dilemma, as shown in the following chapter in which I begin with one of the most mundane problems encountered in aid administration — that of delay.

Delay

It is a rare occurrence for aid projects to be completed on schedule. There are numerous reasons for this, many of which are practical problems of working in a developing country, for example poor transport and communications, and lack of skilled staff or equipment. My concern is not with these, but with other important factors which result from the nature of the aid process itself; I will identify three.

The first is a lack of commitment on the part of the recipient government. Those required to implement the project, with foreign assistance, are simply not sufficiently interested. This might be due to a change of government or of senior personnel between the time when the project is prepared and when it is implemented. More commonly, however, it is because the donor rather than the recipient is the driving force behind the project. This, in turn, may be either because the project involves the exercise of leverage, or because the donor agency, in its attempt to maximise expenditure, encourages the recipient to request a project to which it actually feels little or no commitment. For example, a number of aid agencies are very keen to encourage developing countries to change their housing policies, upgrading slums and shanties rather than destroying them and building expensive houses in their place. Despite the compelling logic of the argument, many countries are resistant to this approach; but the consensus of opinion among donor agencies is so strong that prospective recipient countries find it convenient to accept finance for such slum and shanty upgrading projects. In many cases, however, such is the lack of interest in the recipient country that low priority is in fact attached to the project, and progress is extremely slow.

A slightly different example, also from the housing field, is the case of a site-and-service scheme. In one South Asian country this approach to housing was being actively pursued, and a bilateral agency was keen to assist. The nature of site-and-service schemes, however, is such that the majority of the expenditure is on locally produced items, and salaries. Since the policy of the donor agency was to finance only the foreign exchange component of the total cost, the aid offered was in fact rather small, consisting of sanitary fixtures, nails, bolts etc. The total cost of these items was a very small proportion of the total, whilst the administrative cost of obtaining them was rather high. As a result the government department concerned was not very active in taking advantage of the assistance it had been encouraged to accept. Thus although the project went ahead, the expenditure of aid funds was very slow.

The second cause of delay is dissension within the recipient government regarding the project. The proposal may be accepted by the minister or senior civil servant concerned, but be opposed by another member of staff whose co-operation is essential. For example, aid was promised to a government department on the food-for-work principle, that instead of wages, people should be given food. The total value of the food aid was considerable, and the project was agreed to by the ministry concerned. The head of the relevant department, however, opposed the use of this food as payment for what was intended to be a self-help construction scheme, on the grounds that this would undermine the basic principle of the project (quite apart from the extremely costly and cumbersome procedures involved in importing, storing, transporting and distributing the food). Both the parties concerned were well intentioned and believed themselves to be acting in the people's interest, but in the face of such disagreement, delay, or total inactivity, was inevitable.

The last two examples quoted include reference to what is a third major cause of delay in aid projects — the very cumbersome procedures which have to be followed in order to obtain and spend the funds. Some of these result from the exercise of leverage — for example from procurement tying, or the desire to ensure that the beneficiaries of the project are those intended by the donor. Others arise out of the donor's need to account adequately for its expenditures. (A recipient ministry may be receiving assistance from ten different donor agencies, each with accounting procedures which are not only alien and more demanding than those used by the ministry for its own funds, but also different one from another. The resulting complexity is enormous.) In either case, the rules and regulations surrounding the aid process, compounded by the problems of communication, are a major source of delay.

Lack of Results

The next thing that can happen is that although funds are spent as

planned, none of the expected benefits is realised. The items tested
in the project documents are supplied, but not used. There is no
shortage of examples to cite: tractors that are shipped out to
Africa only to stand rusting and idle; seed going rotten in the stores;
chemicals decomposing as they stand in the warehouses of the port.
These are among the most stark examples of the failures of foreign
aid. How far are they caused by the nature of the aid process?

To a large extent, of course, they are not. The problem is simply
one of inefficiency on the part of the local administration. One
may say that this should be anticipated by the donor agency, and
planned for, but it is not a direct result of the way in which aid is
given.

However, there may also be a lack of commitment, as just discussed, in the case of delay, but this time at a lower level. Thus the
minister and senior civil servants may all be keen to receive the aid,
but the more junior civil servants or community leaders may not be
interested. The aid is in a sense forced upon them, and they make
no effort to take advantage of it.

More often, however, the project is simply ill-conceived. The
failures are most commonly on technical or 'socio-cultural' grounds.
There are many examples of the first type. Snow ploughs actually
were donated to Ghana. Mali was given some sophisticated equipment for installation in a hospital without electricity. Sri Lanka
obtained locomotives that were not powerful enough to carry the
required loads unless used in pairs — and so on.

There are probably many examples of the second type also, but
these are unfortunately less well documented. One well-researched
case was a project in South East Asia where a small whaling
village was provided with new equipment intended to modernise
techniques and increase the size of the catch. Quite apart from the
technical problems encountered it became evident that the social
and cultural aspects of whaling — from the design and construction
of the boats, through the methods of fishing and division of responsibility among the crew to the way in which the catch was distributed — were of paramount importance, and by failing to take
these into account the project ran into severe problems.

One may simply attribute such failures to lack of adequate
planning, which in turn is due to the haste with which projects are

prepared. However, there may also be something wrong with the way in which project 'ideas' are generated. The failings of 'top-down' planning have been much discussed, and I shall return to this question later in this chapter. Here I simply wish to note that in so far as the aid process encourages this type of planning it may be responsible for the socio-cultural, as opposed to the purely technical, errors that are made.

Inequitable Benefits

The next situation I shall consider is where the project is implemented as planned, and yields benefits — but those who gain are not those most in need. (In some instances of course, it is not intended that those most in need shall benefit. My concern here is with the case where those in need are in theory meant to benefit, but in practice do not.) This may be for a number of reasons: because the project is too capital-intensive, or built for prestige reasons; because political patronage determines the selection of the beneficiaries; because an inequitable distribution of gains is built into the method of appraisal. A few examples will provide elucidation.

An international agency hired a team of consultants to appraise a project to construct a sewerage system in a West African city. It soon became evident that the proposed project was inappropriate since the only beneficiaries would be the very few who had piped water supplies in their houses. Not only were these the least needy members of the population, but even they would have to be subsidised to enable the system to be paid for. The two main factors contributing to this situation were a desire for a visible and prestigious project — by recipient as well as prospective donor — and a bias in favour of a capital-intensive project (to which I shall devote a later section of this chapter).

Aid funds are also used to finance the construction of urban roads. But who benefits from such investment? There are some who will suffer during the construction period, and pedestrians may not benefit at all, but road users generally will derive some advantage from the project. Those who gain most, however, are the car owners.

In this type of project the very method of appraisal favours the high income earner. Total benefits of a planned road construction scheme are measured mainly in terms of time savings, vehicle operating cost savings and reduction in accidents. Time savings and accident costs are valued according to the income of the people concerned. Thus the time saved by higher income earners is valued at a higher figure, and there is a corresponding bias in favour of schemes which benefit this group. It is true that, in theory, such benefits can be charged for in the form of tolls so that redistribution of these gains is effected, but this is in practice very rarely done. There is thus a systematic bias caused simply by the methodology used for project appraisal.

A third example relates to public housing schemes. In almost every developing country of the world the public sector has sought to solve its housing problems by building new units, designed to a standard which is considered acceptable, for rent to lower income earners. In practice the national budget is invariably too small to finance more than a small fraction of the number required, and the cost of each unit is so high that it has to be massively subsidised. In a new town in Ghana, for example, the rents charged did not even cover the costs of maintenance, and in many countries the economic rents exceed a typical civil servant's total income. The few people that do enjoy the fruits of such schemes are seldom the most needy, but rather the recipients of political patronage. Thus, the benefits are inequitably distributed. It must be added that this particular example is now becoming outdated. Owing to the manifest failings of such schemes they rarely attract foreign aid nowadays.

In each of the foregoing examples the outcome of the project is that it is medium, or even higher income groups that benefit, and this is all too often the case in foreign aid projects. It is not simply a question of corruption, but rather of a complex set of factors which operate. The 'trickle down' theory of development has long been discredited; the recipient matter has proved unporous, and the bottom layer has waited in vain for even a drop. The evidence for this has caused aid agencies to reconsider their policies and some have sought to exert leverage in order to avoid this situation; but leverage, as we have seen, brings with it other problems.

Unwanted Side Effects

I turn now to the aid project which has side effects which are un-
foreseen and in some way detrimental. One of the most famous
examples is still a matter of dispute. The Aswan Dam provides huge
storage of the Nile waters and thus ensures a reliable and con-
trollable source of irrigation water to millions of acres in Egypt.
But it also prevents the passage of the valuable silts that used to be
washed down and enrich the land, and now have to be replaced by
fertiliser. In addition, the increased incidence of bilharzia in Egypt
has been attributed to this massive project.

Another example is provided by schemes in areas such as the
Sahel, to construct water points for cattle. Unless these are
sufficient in number and carefully located they can lead to overgrazing and denudation of the land. Improved veterinary control,
unless accompanied by measures to increase the rate of offtake,
can also lead to an excess cattle population and hence overgrazing.

But can these problems be attributed to the nature of the aid
process? There are three ways in which such a claim might be sub-
stantiated. First, that aid projects are undertaken in haste, without
sufficient study of their possible consequences. Secondly, that the
desire that projects be 'visible' favours large, prestige schemes.
Thirdly, that there is, for other reasons, a capital bias in the
selection and design of projects. This last point I shall take up later
in the chapter, restricting my discussion here to the first two.

If projects go wrong, it is common, in retrospect, to argue that
insufficient planning was done. Sometimes, such criticisms are made
even while the project is being prepared — as, for example, with the
massive Mahaveli irrigation and power project in Sri Lanka in which
the time scale has been cut from thirty years to six, thus drastically
reducing the possibility of detailed planning. On the other hand, an
average period of ten years from conception to completion, as on
World Bank projects, can hardly be described as hasty — and to
allow more time and money for environmental impact studies, as is
now happening, will further lengthen the process.

With regard to the second point, it is undoubtedly the case that
massive, prestige projects, have great appeal, especially to politicians
(in both donor and recipient countries). It is not necessarily the case

that massive projects are *per se* to be avoided despite the validity of many of the 'small is beautiful' arguments but it is true that with smaller scale comes increased flexibility, and hence the opportunity to adapt the original plan with experience; an option which is less likely to occur in the case of a massive construction project.

What has to be asked in connection with both of these issues is whether the situation is worse than it would be in the absence of foreign aid. Many Third World governments are in more haste than their donors, and their predilection for large, prestige projects is frequently greater. Without foreign aid, they are therefore just as likely to make these errors — if not more so. Aid can therefore be blamed only in so far as it increases the volume of funds available with which, perhaps, to make mistakes.

Maintenance

This is another extremely common problem in development projects. A new water supply is built to provide piped, treated water to the populace. Within a few years, or even months, the pumps break down, or the chlorine runs out, or the operator in charge is given another job. At best this means that the project was a waste of money since the people return to using their wells as before. It may be, however, that the people are actually worse off. If water continues to be pumped but not treated then those connected to the system are receiving polluted water, possibly more injurious to health than their untreated well water.

To give another example from my experience: cattle dips are built and the people encouraged to dip their cattle. After a few years those in charge begin to lose interest, or the transport of dip liquid becomes a problem. So the cattle are no longer treated. At best the situation is as before. However, the cattle may now have less resistance to the diseases concerned, so that the net effect of the project is actually detrimental.

Why do such situations come about? It is not simply a question of inefficiency or laziness. There is something inherent in the rules of aid-giving that increase the likelihood of this sort of problem.

Governments typically differentiate in their budgets between capital and recurrent expenditures. It is clearly most important to maintain an appropriate balance between the two, but what is 'appropriate' in any given situation cannot be defined in general terms, and certainly not in terms of a specified ratio. The dangers of imbalance can be demonstrated by reference to a few examples. The most obvious, perhaps, is that there is no point in spending money on new cars if you cannot afford to maintain them. With a given stock of cars a balance must be struck between buying more cars and ensuring that funds are available for petrol, spares, drivers etc. to make use of those that already exist.

Similarly, but perhaps less obviously, there is no point in building new schools if you cannot afford to staff them; there is no point in providing new hospital equipment if you cannot afford the electricity to operate it; new roads without sufficient funds to repair them on a permanent maintenance basis are a waste of money, and so on.

It is frequently the case that capital expenditure is excessive in relation to recurrent. There are a number of reasons why this is so. Capital expenditure (or investment) is more closely associated with 'development' — indeed the term 'development budget' is often used instead of capital budget. Government departments are sometimes even divided into two parts — one concerned with day-to-day management and the other with development. It is not surprising that it is the latter which attracts more interest, and more capable and ambitious staff. Capital expenditure is more 'visible'; politicians and others are likely to spend money on things which have glamour. Thus the construction of a new road has more appeal than the repair of an old one. Or, to take a more extreme but perfectly true example, one may choose to build a new water treatment plant rather than to train and employ a much needed water treatment technician.

These types of problems are exacerbated by the provision of development aid. With regard to the previous example quoted, a donor agency would not, in general, even consider providing the funds to employ a skilled maintenance technician, but would be all too willing to finance the construction of a new treatment plant. The reasons for this seem logical in context, but their effect is to increase the imbalance between capital and recurrent expenditure.

Most donor agencies simply do not allow project expenditure on recurrent costs. There are some ways of getting round this, for example by 'capitalising' certain items for a short period of time, and some agencies are becoming more flexible in this regard. But the rule is generally, and strictly, applied.

There are a number of reasons — discussed in the following chapter — why donor agencies are so resistant to recurrent cost financing. The resulting bias in expenditure towards the capital budget reduces the relative expenditure on maintenance, with, in many cases, damaging and wasteful effects.

Profligate Use of Capital and Foreign Exchange

It was, and to a large extent still is, common practice for donor agencies to meet only the foreign exchange component of the capital costs of a project. The practical justification for meeting only capital costs has just been discussed; but there is also a more ideological reason, albeit rather vague. This is associated with the belief that aid is not a permanent measure. A day will come, it is argued, when poor countries are sufficiently rich to be able to dispense with aid. This will happen as the result of investment, not consumption, and aid should be restricted to projects which will eventually lead to the recipient country's self-reliance. Thus for ideological as well as practical reasons, aid should be used for capital and not for recurrent expenditure.

In addition, often only the foreign exchange component is met by the donor. In the case of tied aid it is not hard to see why this is so; but the policy is often also defended where aid, although not tied, is still restricted to foreign exchange costs. The argument goes that the recipient country must demonstrate its interest in, and commitment to, the project by meeting the local costs. This will not only ensure that it participates fully in the implementation of the project, but will also reduce the paternalistic, 'free hand-out' attitude to aid which is damaging to both recipient and donor.

While there is certainly something in this argument, the same objective could be achieved by other means, which would thereby avoid the distorting effect of this policy which can be most serious. Take, for example, the sectoral bias that results, which I have already mentioned in the chapter on leverage. Agriculture is at a distinct disadvantage by comparison with, say transport, since the capital component of projects in the latter sector is typically higher, as is the foreign exchange component. A similar bias operates in favour of certain types of project and, of course, the choice of technique is considerably distorted.

A few examples may be useful. In Sri Lanka, there has been for many years a programme to improve sanitation in rural areas by encouraging householders to replace their pit latrines with 'sanitary latrines', designed and located so as to minimise the danger of faecal pollution. Householders are given a small grant towards the cost of construction, a squatting plate, and assistance with design if necessary. It is an extremely difficult project to administer, since it covers a huge area and the amounts of materials and money involved for each household are small. It is, however, potentially a very good programme, which would achieve great benefits at little cost. Yet it is extremely unattractive to foreign aid donors: largely because the capital costs and the foreign exchange costs are very small.

In Ecuador, a study was undertaken so as to identify how best to increase the capacity of the ports. It became evident, as in many studies, that by more efficient management the volume of goods handled could be greatly increased without building additional quays or warehouses. Indeed, if ships were also unloaded via barges it would be several years before major additional construction was required. But such a solution would involve little capital expenditure and little foreign exchange. This was one of the reasons why such a solution was not adopted.

There are many other such cases. The Overseas Development Institute undertook a number of studies of the impact of British aid to a number of African countries. The following quotation summarises some of their conclusions: 'First, donor preferences for aiding large capital projects (preferences not entirely at odds with the recipient government's own tastes) combined with their reluctance to finance local costs, helped to create a 'development' programme dominated by such projects.'[1]

In analysing the behaviour of ministries in the recipient country it is necessary to distinguish between civil servants in the Treasury and in the line ministries, as noted in Chapter 4. While the former will be concerned with the terms on which aid is given (favouring grants rather than loans for example) the latter will wish to maximise their total aid receipts, and may give scant consideration to repayment terms. With recipient line ministries trying to maximise their receipts, while donors seek to spend their aid budgets subject to these policies, it is not surprising that the bar on recurrent and local cost financing often results in projects being designed so as to maximise their foreign exchange and their capital components.

But developing countries are generally typified by their lack of capital and of foreign exchange. Indeed these are frequently identified as the major constraints to economic development. This is reflected in the early work on project appraisal techniques, which still influences the theory if not the practice of project design and selection. This emphasised the importance of these constraints and suggested that both capital and foreign exchange were often undervalued in developing countries, so that market prices failed to reflect their true scarcity. Techniques of appraisal were, therefore, designed to counteract these distortions; but they failed to do so (largely because of the excessive expectations of what economic techniques, and over-sophisticated ones at that, could achieve in the face of such strong counteracting forces).

Thus, despite the fact that capital and foreign exchange are generally in short supply in the developing countries, and despite the fact that appraisal techniques adopted by many donor agencies nominally take account of this in their project design and selection, there is a strong tendency for foreign aid projects to be biased towards the use of capital and of foreign exchange.

Lack of Skilled Manpower

That lack of skilled manpower is one of the major problems of developing countries is a commonplace. It may seem strange, however, to suggest that development aid may actually exacerbate the problem, for development assistance not only finances training but also the provision of advisers and consultants. Although there are many shortcomings in such assistance, it does result in an increase in skills available to the recipient country.

I am concerned, however, with three ways in which donors may reduce the skilled manpower available. First, by sending people abroad for foreign training they increase the likelihood of their staying abroad, or subsequently emigrating in search of employment. A qualified doctor, for example, can earn incomparably more in Europe than in India — even if he worked as a garage attendant. I shall discuss in Chapter 6 whether such migration is in fact detrimental, since it has certain compensating benefits, but the 'brain drain' is certainly regarded as a problem in many poor countries — and can in part be attributed to the assistance provided by foreign aid donors to enable the most skilled people to travel and study abroad.

Secondly, many aid agencies employ people from developing countries. This is always financially advantageous to those employed, and often very beneficial to the aid projects, since it ensures that the aid agency can make use of local knowledge (or almost local knowledge — the incongruous situation used to hold that the UN, which employs many experts from developing countries, especially those with numerous graduates such as India and Egypt, was not able to use such experts in the one country where they are most knowledgeable — their own). Although in most respects it is entirely desirable that aid agencies should employ people from developing countries, this does nevertheless cause a further drain on the highest levels of skilled manpower.

Thirdly, aid agencies, and particularly the banks, are keen to ensure the success of the projects they finance, both in the interests of the recipient country and themselves. As a result it is not uncommon for them to insist that certain guarantees be made with regard to staffing. They sometimes seek to create new and more autonomous organisations, concerned, for example, with water supply or electricity. In order to ensure that these are well staffed they drain other organisations of some of their most competent personnel, by offering better conditions or higher salaries. While this does not reduce the total manpower available, it may distort its distribution in a manner detrimental to the interests of the country as a whole.

In summary, it is generally the case that aid increases rather than reduces the total skilled manpower availability in developing countries, but by virtue of the way in which aid is given there are certain important ways in which this beneficial effect is offset.

The Formation of an Alien Elite

I have already discussed the problems that may arise as a result of projects being planned, and perhaps largely implemented, by foreigners who are insufficiently aware of local socio-cultural conditions. There is a distinct but closely related problem, namely, that the aid process can contribute to the formation of an elite class within the recipient country, whose values are more closely akin to those of the administrators of aid than their compatriots on whose behalf they are planning. I am concerned here not with the problem of benefits being inequitably distributed as a result, (which has already been discussed) but with the widening gap that opens up between the people of the recipient country and those who represent them, in terms of their values and hence their understanding of what constitute priority needs.

As an illustration of the problem let me quote the case of a cattle ranching project in the north of Tanzania assisted by foreign finance. The scheme involved a tribe of traditional pastoralists, the Masai, for whom cattle are not only a store of wealth, but have a significance which goes far beyond that of a mere source of income. One of the aims of the project was to improve veterinary standards and hence reduce death rates. There was a danger, however, that the resulting increase in cattle population would lead to overgrazing. In order to graze the land at its optimal level, and possibly even increase its carrying capacity, it was essential to increase the offtake rate (i.e. the proportion of the herd sold for slaughter each year) which would thereby increase the income of the Masai.

The Masai, however, although welcoming improved veterinary services did not necessarily want to raise the rate of offtake.

Indeed they saw the benefit of the project largely as increasing their herd sizes. In order to try and encourage them to change this attitude, shops were to be introduced into the area, selling goods which they might be tempted to buy, such as radios and bicycles. It was anticipated that the Masai would gradually be induced to sell more cattle in order to be able to buy these goods.

In this case, as it happened, some of the local project staff expressed concern at the approach, which was based on the assumption that the values of the Masai had to be changed in their own best interest. Other cases could be cited where local staff are unaware of the extent to which they are imposing or imputing alien values.

Housing projects offer a good example. It is quite common in developing countries for houses designed and built by the public sector to be more like houses in the West than those in their own country, which have developed in accordance with the needs and preferences of the people as well as utilising locally available materials. Thus not only may imported materials be used, but the layout of the houses and the method of construction are often ill-suited, both climatically and culturally, to the local conditions. Ironically, aid agencies are becoming increasingly aware of this and often seek to encourage civil servants, against their inclinations, to allow the use of, for example, reinforced mud brick for construction, and to design the houses to take account of the local cultural conditions (by providing for more than just the nuclear family, encouraging the use of open space etc.).

An awareness of the problem on the donor side stems partly from the experience of city planners in the West who have, in recent decades, become concerned at the fact that they are imposing their 'middle-class values' on those for whom they plan. Clearly the gap in the case of aid projects is far wider. How can a city-dwelling, Christian, university educated, salary-earning engineer, for example, have any idea of the needs and priorities of a Bedouin tribesman or an Indian peasant? Yet it may well be the case that the former is not a foreign aid administrator but a local civil servant. The gap is thus not between those in the donor and recipient agencies but between the local educated elite, who make the decisions, and the mass of the population, on whose behalf they are made.

The aid process can exacerbate this problem, because through aid the decision makers in the recipient countries come into increasing contact with the values and traditions of an alien culture, and come, very often, to adopt these as their own, becoming as a result increasingly separated from the people whom they are meant to represent, and correspondingly ill-equipped to plan on their behalf.

Conclusion

As indicated earlier, this does not constitute an exhaustive list of all the possible criticisms of aid, but it does identify the major practical problems which limit the effectiveness of aid, and which can, in large part, be attributed to the way in which the aid process works.

Most of these problems are interrelated. Some reinforce each other, so that capital-bias in choice of technology, for example, is compounded by lack of maintenance because of shortage of recurrent funds. Others are inversely related, so that the more time is spent on trying to foresee possible deleterious side effects of a project, the more it is delayed.

Most of these problems, I assert, can be traced back to the donor's desire to exercise control over the way aid is used — whether from self-interested motives or in an attempt to ensure the effective implementation of the project by building in safe-guards against the anticipated folly or venality of the politicians and civil servants of the recipient country.

In view of the enormous problems that result from this policy, it has to be challenged. Is it possible that the cure is worse than the disease? If the complex machinery of aid were largely dismembered, what would be the outcome? Those who defend the present system would no doubt claim that chaos would result from the incom-petence and corruption of the recipients. Let me consider these two possibilities in turn.

Very frequently, but by no means always, the technical com-petence of the foreign 'expert', whether planning or implementing a project, is greater than that of the local person who would otherwise be responsible. However, the foreigner's ignorance of local political conditions (and, not withstanding my earlier argument, of socio-cultural conditions also) largely offsets any advantage in technical know-how.

Secondly, the provision of foreign expertise increases dependency and defers the day when the recipient country becomes self-sufficient in manpower. In order to learn, it is necessary to take responsibility and make mistakes, and unless recipients are allowed to do so they will never cease to rely on aid. At present those who learn by their mistakes are largely those from the donor countries, who thereby become better experts — at the expense of those who could benefit most.

A more insurmountable problem is that of corruption. Donors fear that unless they exercise some control over the disbursement of aid funds these will be put to the use of politicians eager to increase their status and electoral support, and that politicians, civil servants, contractors and others may take the opportunity to 'cream off' a portion of the money that passes through their hands. While such claims are often exaggerated, it is a more compelling argument than that of incompetence, and deserves the more lengthy treatment which I shall give in the next chapter.

Notes

1. Rob Wood and Kathryn Morton, 'Has British Aid Helped Poor Countries? — Five African Cases', *ODI Review*, no. I (1977).

6 ALTERNATIVES

In this chapter I shall be concerned with ways of improving the aid process so as to reduce or altogether avoid the problems outlined earlier. But there is also the possibility of replacing aid by some other strategy aimed at achieving the same end. I shall briefly consider three such alternatives.

Trade

The first is to concentrate on trade instead of aid. Developing countries have three main concerns with regard to trade. The first is the level of prices: it is claimed (and generally conceded) that there has been a downward trend in the prices of primary products, other than oil, relative to the prices of manufactured goods, since about 1950. The second concern is the instability of prices of individual commodities, leading to problems of economic management in the exporting countries. The third is tariffs, quotas and other forms of protection imposed by rich countries to exclude the manufactured goods of developing countries. Debate over these issues has been continuing for many years, with UNCTAD serving as a major forum, and the positions taken up by the various interest groups have become increasingly polarised.

The precise nature of the problem of trade however, varies quite widely between exporting countries. Some are disproportionately dependent on a single commodity e.g. Zambia where copper accounts for over 90 per cent of exports, Gambia (over 80 per cent groundnuts), Cuba and Mauritius (over 80 per cent sugar). Others, such as Brazil or Singapore, are more concerned about import quotas limiting their exports of textiles or other manufactured goods.

Various measures have been proposed to alleviate these problems. On some issues there seems to be almost direct conflict of interest between exporter and importer — for example with regard to protection — and little agreement is reached. On the issue of price stabilisation, however, the mutuality of interest is clearer, and measures such as the Common Fund and the setting up of International Commodity Agreements have had some success.

The 'trade not aid' argument states, very simply, that the interests of poor countries would be better served not by aid but the adoption of measures to raise and stabilise the prices of primary products and allow greater access, particularly for manufactured goods, to the markets of the rich countries.

The rich countries generally choose to make a very clear distinction between the two issues, and adopt a hard-nosed approach to trade negotiations. Unless the arguments of the Brandt Commission regarding the mutuality of interests prevail, the rich countries are likely to continue to maintain this position.

Investment

The second alternative is that poor countries should have access to the capital markets of the rich countries which, instead of providing aid, would concentrate on commercial bank loans and foreign investment, whether by state or private enterprise. Although this is a view more commonly put forward by the developed countries, it is not without support among at least the richer of the developing countries. This indicates the major problem of such an approach. To quote the Brandt report:

> Foreign investment has moved to a limited number of developing countries, mainly those which could offer political stability and a convenient economic environment, including tax incentives, large markets, cheap labour and easy access to oil or other natural resources. Purely financial investments have gone to tax havens in the developing countries which the UN lists as Bahamas, Barbados, Cayman Islands, Netherlands, Antilles, and Panama. Of the rest, 70 per cent of the investment in the Third World has

been in only fifteen countries. Over 20 per cent is in Brazil and Mexico alone and the rest in other middle-income countries in Latin America — Argentina, Peru, Venezuela — or in South-East Asia — Malaysia, Singapore, Hong Kong. About one-quarter is in oil-exporting developing countries. In the poorer countries foreign investment is mainly in plantations and minerals, or in countries with large internal markets — like India. Private investment can supplement and complement aid, but it cannot substitute for it: it tends not to move to the countries or sectors which most need aid.[1]

There are thus two problems with replacing aid by commercial loans and foreign investment. First, there is resistance from prospective recipient countries, wary of exploitation and loss of sovereignty. Secondly, such a strategy would provide funds to only a few, relatively advanced countries — not the many which are most in need but have little to offer in terms of low risk returns for the investor.

It is ironic, in view of this, that in recent years it is these types of financial flows that have been increasing most rapidly. In 1960, more than 60 per cent of total foreign funds to the developing countries came from concessional aid or official development assistance. By 1977 this figure had fallen to one-third. The remainder was commercial, mainly from private bank loans, direct investment and export credits.

Migration

A third alternative to aid is migration. Temporary or illegal migration between countries is an extremely important phenomenon. In several European countries, most notably Germany, 10 per cent or even 20 per cent of the labour force is composed of migrant labour, from countries such as Algeria, Turkey and Yugoslavia. The oil-rich countries of the Middle East rely heavily on migrants from Pakistan and other parts of Asia. The United States employs millions of Mexicans, mainly as farm workers. In South Africa the mines are full of workers from neighbouring countries.

Before national boundaries were fixed, migration of a permanent nature could offer the solution to countries with inadequate resources to support their population. Today, it is not so simple. Mali's problems of increasing population combined with steady desertification are, it is true, eased by the movement of Malians to the Ivory Coast in search of work. But a massive and continuing permanent migration from poor countries to richer would be strongly resisted by the rich countries — even if it were acceptable as a matter of national policy by the countries from which they depart.

Clearly migration is of financial benefit to the migrant, but if it is to be compared to aid in the narrowly defined sense (i.e. in terms of nations rather than people) it is necessary also to ask how far it will benefit the migrant's country of origin. On the one hand there are the migrant's remittances while abroad and the acquired skills and savings when he or she eventually returns home. Against this must be set the expenditure, by the country of origin, on education.

The total amount received in remittances from abroad can be very substantial. In Jordan and Sri Lanka, for example, a large proportion of total export earnings come from this source, both from skilled and unskilled labour. In the case of the former the costs of education, and, even more important, the potential value of such educated personnel, may be considerable. The 'brain drain' is therefore an issue of major importance. Can such countries afford to lose so many able and talented people when there is a desperate need for their services at home? There can be little doubt that if costs are measured only in terms of investment in education then the benefits from remittances and from the migrant's eventual return generally more than compensate. But when viewed in the context of the constraint to the country's development resulting from the loss of such talent the case is far less clear-cut.

The question thus arises whether it would be better to allow and encourage more migration rather than to rely on aid. In view of the present strength of national feeling in the world, it is unrealistic to propose that major permanent shifts of population should occur. But increased temporary migration, with adequate safeguards and terms of employment for the migrants, could well offer a viable alternative to aid.

A number of other measures are commonly proposed in discussions of the problems of poor countries — most recently in the Report of the Brandt Commission. Some of these have no place in the present discussion because they could not replace aid, but might complement it. Population control, for example, is considered by many to be vital, but it would at best serve to mitigate tomorrow's problems, not solve today's, and cannot therefore be regarded as an alternative to aid.

World monetary reforms, also, should belooked upon as complementary to aid rather than as substitutes, with the possible exception of the so-called 'SDR link'. It is proposed that SDRs (Special Drawing Rights) should become the principal reserve asset in the international monetary system. In so far as this led to an orderly increase in world liquidity it would gain support from many countries. It has also been suggested, however, that these SDRs should be distributed in a manner which favoured the poor countries. While the Brandt Report, for example, maintains that this would be justified on grounds of efficiency as well as equity, others would regard this as simply another form of resource transfer from rich to poor, albeit a relatively painless one.

This concludes my brief summary of alternatives to aid. I now turn to the question of what changes might be made in the way in which aid is given i.e. less radical modifications which are based on the premiss that aid needs to be altered, not done away with entirely.

The common underlying feature of these proposals, and indeed much of the analysis of this book, raises the fundamental question of whether it is not time to change the nature of the aid relationship itself. Instead of slowly conceding ground with regard to specific 'rules of the game' is it not time to allow aid recipients a voice in drawing up the rules? This is the question I shall address at the end of this chapter. First I shall discuss more modest proposals.

Many of these involve merely tinkering with the present system and indeed are already being discussed, and in some cases implemented, by aid donors. So long as the aid relationship is unequal, and control remains with the donors, only relatively minor changes

such as those discussed may be realistically considered. As I shall
show, however, many of these changes could nevertheless be
beneficial, and it is to be hoped that they will be accepted.

Financing Recurrent Costs

The first proposal is that donors should be more prepared to finance
the recurrent costs of aid projects. This would have two advantages.
First, it would reduce the capital bias in the selection of projects
and the technology adopted for implementing them. Prospective
recipients would not be tempted, as they are at present, to try and
maximise the total amount of aid received by choosing projects
and techniques which maximise the capital, and hence foreign-
funded, component.

Secondly it might encourage recipients to use aid funds to repair
rather than replace existing capital items. This is generally far more
cost-effective. In addition, greater efficiency will be achieved if a
more appropriate balance can be struck between recurrent and
capital funds (e.g. for buying petrol to run the cars that the
ministry already owns rather than buying new ones which cannot
be used for lack of petrol).

But donors are often resistant to financing recurrent costs. One
reason that is given derives from the view that aid funds must be
used to stimulate economic growth which, it is argued, will result
from productive investment, not from consumption expenditure;
therefore aid funds must be channelled into investment (i.e.
capital expenditure) rather than consumption (i.e. recurrent
expenditure). While the emphasis on economic growth may be unexceptionable, the assumption that capital expenditure is
necessarily productive, and recurrent funds are spent only on
consumption is too simplistic.

A second argument is that apart from the salaries of consultants
and advisers (which donors are usually happy to finance), most
recurrent costs involve no foreign exchange component. This
raises problems which I shall be discussing below, in the context
of local cost funding.

There are, however, three other considerations which may also carry some weight with aid donors. The first is that it is more difficult to monitor recurrent expenditure than capital expenditure, and hence to guarantee that funds are spent as the donor would wish. Secondly, a commitment to finance recurrent costs tends to be rather open-ended, whereas aid donors prefer to provide their assistance as a series of discrete and bounded projects. Thirdly, recurrent expenditure is less visible than capital expenditure. Although the effects of the former may be far more beneficial, it does not have the same publicity effect as, say, the donation of a hospital or a dam. This last consideration is pertinent to aid recipients as well, but they are generally more likely to favour recurrent cost financing by donors.

Financing Local Costs

The next proposal, that donors should be more willing to finance the local cost component of projects and programmes, is closely related to the question of recurrent cost financing; but the two issues must be distinguished since recurrent costs may nevertheless require foreign exchange (and, conversely, capital items may be purchased locally). In addition, the arguments for and against local cost funding are somewhat different from those regarding recurrent costs.

First, such a policy would reduce the import bias in the technology selected for projects, which results partly from recipients (and donors) attempting to increase aid by maximising the foreign exchange component of aid projects. This in turn would tend both to reduce the capital intensity of techniques selected, and also problems of repair and maintenance of equipment.

Secondly, and perhaps more importantly, the import bias in the selection of projects would also be reduced. It is undoubtedly the case that developing countries include projects in their Development Plans with an eye to attracting foreign aid. Those projects with very low foreign exchange costs are less likely to appeal to donors, and also to the recipient country which may feel that the time and effort involved in obtaining aid, and the strings attached to its use, outweigh its benefit where it accounts for only a small proportion of total cost. There is therefore a tendency for project selection as well as choice of technology to be biased by the desire of recipients to attract aid.

Donors have in the past tended to resist local cost financing, and are changing their policies only rather slowly. One of their major arguments has been that aid must be a collaborative exercise, and the recipient must be actively involved in any projects undertaken; the extent of commitment of the recipient government being indicated by its willingness to contribute to total costs.

However, there are also other considerations — some of which are similar to those relating to recurrent cost funding. Thus, monitoring of local costs can be more difficult for the donor. The visibility of aid, and the opportunity to advertise the donor country's products are reduced, and, of course, if funds are spent locally they cannot be 'tied', so that opportunities for exports of goods and services from the donor country are reduced.

While recipients generally favour having the option of local cost financing, there are certain technical problems involved in converting foreign exchange, and some countries are anxious about allowing donors the opportunity to hold large quantities of funds in local currency.

Programme not Project Aid

In recent years some aid donors have been shifting towards programme rather than project aid. That is to say that they are prepared to offer aid which may be used for any approved purpose within an overall programme agreed by the donor and recipient such as, for example, rural water supply or the development of a particular district. This generally involves a more flexible attitude both to recurrent cost and local cost financing, as well as relaxing some of the controls over the precise use to which funds are put, at least within a broad framework. The merits of this approach will, I hope, become increasingly recognised by other donors, but since it incorporates a number of the alternative measures I am discussing in this chapter it is not necessary to deal with it as a separate proposal.

Untying Aid

There are two major advantages to be gained by untying aid, i.e. allowing recipients to purchase their required goods and services from any source, not necessarily from the donor country. The first is that this reduces costs. As has already been noted, it has been estimated that the tying of aid can increase costs by at least as much as 20 per cent, and even so the quality of the product may be poor and, in the case of equipment, it may be incompatible with other items in use. In addition, the problem of spare parts is minimised if aid is untied. The difficulty of maintaining machinery and equipment has already been discussed; this can be enormously exacerbated if every aid donor requires that their own firms should supply the goods they finance, leading to a multiplicity of different pieces of equipment, a far greater stock-holding requirement, delays and increased costs.

Bilateral donors are understandably rather resistant to the untying of aid, since they fear it leads to a loss of export earnings, if not actually boosting the sales of competing countries. Therefore it is not surprising that many of them oppose the suggestion. But in view of the manifest benefits of untying they are subject to increasing pressure from bodies such as the Development Assistance Committee of OECD, according to whose 1979 Review 'the majority (ten) of DAC donors have accepted the DAC memorandum on untying of bilateral development loans in favour of procurement in developing countries.'[2] Nevertheless roughly 40 per cent of total aid is available only for procurement in the respective donor country. There is thus still a long way to go.

Multilateral not Bilateral Aid

Another alternative measure is to abandon bilateral aid altogether, replacing it entirely by assistance channelled through multilateral agencies. The most important reason to do so would be to do away with, or at least greatly reduce, the exertion of leverage by donors in their own commercial, strategic or political interest. The issue of leverage has already been discussed at length in this book, and requires no further elaboration. But there are some other merits in replacing bilateral by multilateral aid.

These relate to the efficiency of the aid process. By reducing the number of aid donors it might be possible to reduce the amount of time spent, and largely wasted, in negotiations and discussions by senior-level local staff. Secondly, the donors would be able to build up a greater knowledge of the recipient country and hence be better equipped to identify and appraise good projects. Thirdly, the lack of coordination, and indeed lack of co-operation between some donors would be reduced, one hopes (although the degree of competition between some international agencies sometimes appears to be just as intense as that between bilateral donors). The terms and conditions of aid and the procedures to be followed would also be more standardised, leading to some saving in time.

Donors are clearly rather ambivalent about the idea, since they channel a part but never all their total aid funds through multilateral agencies (the proportion varying from very little to more than half). Clearly they are reluctant to lose control over the way in which funds are used, although recognising the merits of multilateral aid. Perhaps their willingness to support multilateral agencies can be taken as an indicator of the relative importance of the different considerations which motivate them to provide assistance.

Recipient countries do not necessarily prefer multilateral agencies. Not only do they tend to become more actively involved in the details of domestic economic policy, they may also be more demanding in their application of strict banking criteria. In addition, any reduction in the number of donors reduces the possibility of playing one off against another.

Recipient countries may feel the same about aid consortia, i.e. groups of donor countries which meet, often under the chairmanship of the World Bank, to coordinate their aid programmes to a certain country. Clearly this practice can lead to better coordination, and offers a compromise between bilateral and multilateral funding. Aid recipients, may, however, feel rather threatened by an annual gathering whose purpose appears to be to evaluate their economic performance, and, by actions if not always in words, pass judgement upon it.

Although in principle it would certainly be better for aid to be channelled through multilateral rather than bilateral agencies, the advantages of this policy would in fact be assured only if some of the other changes proposed in this chapter were also put into effect.

Country or Sector Concentration

Many multilateral agencies specialise in particular sectors or types of project e.g. the Food and Agriculture Organisation, or the World Health Organisation, and bilateral donors tend to concentrate their efforts on particular countries which they favour or in sectors in which they have a particular interest or expertise. But there is still very considerable scope for increased specialisation and concentration. This could lead to the same sorts of benefits that would be derived from other alternatives already discussed: greater knowledge of particular countries and sectors and hence greater ability to identify and prepare projects; less time wasted by recipient agencies with a multiplicity of different aid donors; and fewer problems of lack of coordination between them.

Bilateral agencies are often favourably inclined to such a policy, which is followed in theory, but tends to become eroded by events. Thus, a visit by a Head of State may lead to the promise of aid to a country which is not listed as priority; a zealous project identification mission may be impressed by a specific request for aid in a sector in which the donor is not traditionally involved; and so on.

Among bilateral donors a certain amount of country and sector concentration undoubtedly occurs. This results not only from official statements of policy by the various donors, and observation by others of their patterns of allocation, but also from formal and informal discussions between them at international meetings, such as the aid consortia, and during missions to prospective recipient countries. But the sectoral specialisation which should obtain among multilateral agencies is often sadly lacking. In a field such as urban development, for example, there are a number of different UN agencies which stake their claim and, at the risk of duplication, undertake projects and organise international conferences along very similar lines.

From the recipient point of view there is much to be said for donor specialisation. Not only does it increase the experience and competence of the donors, it also reduces the number of different missions that have to be entertained and provided with information. But it also, of course, reduces the number of prospective donors, if not the total amount of their aid, and as already mentioned, may therefore reduce the extent to which one can be played off against another.

Continuity within the Recipient Country

There is an unfortunate tendency for aid donors to abandon one project or type of project and shift their efforts to another in the same country. This means that the experience they have gained, probably through making a number of mistakes, is largely wasted, while the new project is just as likely to run into other problems, as yet unanticipated. It is partly because of the unreasonable optimism which pervades most project documents that the reality is so disappointing. Nevertheless, the experience is still, at least in most cases, of value, not only in what has been achieved, but also in what has been learnt. It is, therefore, a pity that donors so frequently prefer to change to a different project, region or sector, rather than to develop a more successful follow-up to their first, perhaps much criticised scheme. Not only would this increase the likelihood of a follow-up project's being successful, it would also allow the donors to ensure that the operation and maintenance stage of the first project goes smoothly.

It is not surprising that donors are resistant to such an approach. Not only is it more interesting and more effective in terms of 'visibility' to keep starting new schemes, it is also easier to walk away from controversial and difficult projects than to try and sort them out.

On the other hand donors are quite right to avoid the situation in which they simply take over all responsibility for a programme, a sector, a town or a region. As a result, however, they often go too far in the opposite direction, and switch from one to another with such rapidity that no opportunity arises to learn from past mistakes and build up expertise.

Improved Project Identification and Preparation

Clearly all donors favour improving their methods of project identification and preparation, but it is far from clear how this can be achieved. The usual approach is simply to increase the time, effort and expertise invested in these stages of the aid process: to employ more economists, engineers, planners and other experts to carry out more preparatory studies. In so far as this is simply more of the same it cannot be considered an alternative, but there is a way in which the nature of these exercises might be changed.

The process of identification of the project might focus directly on the prospective beneficiaries by identifying a particular area or sector of the country and asking the people concerned to specify their needs and priorities, and to involve them actively in the process of project preparation. One method is for one or more anthropologists, or members of other disciplines prepared to adopt the methods of participant observation, to spend several months or even years in the area concerned and discover the needs and wants of the population simply by living among them. Clearly, project identification would then become a more lengthy process, although the costs involved might be no greater.

Another alternative is more akin to the community participation and 'bottom-up' planning approach, whereby the donor has meetings with representatives of the community at a very early stage, perhaps even the first stage, of the project identification process. Thereafter community involvement is encouraged, and project preparation is largely under the control of local leaders. This method is being increasingly tried by aid donors, dissatisfied with the traditional methods, but recipient agencies are often resistant because this is seen as bypassing the proper channels of government. Politicians may wonder who will take the credit for what their people receive, and even feel their authority and power undermined.

Use of Non-governmental Organisations

An alternative which has some of the merits of this approach, without necessarily incurring the criticism of the recipient agencies, is the use of non-governmental organisations.

At present only about one-tenth of total aid comes from private sources, but donor agencies are taking an increasing interest in the use of non-governmental organisations as channels for their funds. These may be national or international organisations, having a base in the prospective recipient country concerned. Such organisations often have close ties at local community level, and relatively high levels of skill in comparison with the resources at their command. They thus offer the opportunity of alleviating the problem of absorptive capacity which is most serious in the poorest countries. They may also be more effective in the case of projects requiring active community participation, which is hard to achieve with the usual aid process involving visiting experts from the donor country and local government officials. In addition, in cases where aid donors are particularly concerned about corruption — whether for personal financial gain, or the use of aid to gain political support — they may prefer to use non-governmental organisations in the expectation that the risk is then reduced.

Recipient countries, however, may be less keen since such a system excludes the government to a large extent from the decision-making process. Whether they doubt the competence of such organisations, or because they would prefer the credit derived from aid to reflect on themselves, recipient governments do not always favour this approach.

The non-governmental organisations themselves may also be ambivalent. While access to more funds obviously increases their scope, they may hesitate to become closely linked either to the government or the donor country, and prefer to retain their independence, even at the cost of forgoing financial support.

The range of non-governmental organisations is, of course, extremely wide. At one extreme there are the huge international ones like OXFAM, Save the Children, CARE, and so on, including those affiliated with specific religions. At the other extreme are small local bodies which may be community associations of one kind or another. Clearly the stated, and unstated, aims of such organisations are of importance in deciding whether they constitute an acceptable channel for aid funds, both from donor and recipient's point of view, even if the principle of using non-governmental organisations is adopted.

The administrative effort involved in setting up a project through non-governmental organisations may be considerable compared to the amount of money involved, but the success of the scheme is likely to be greatly enhanced. For this reason it is to be hoped that this alternative will also gain wider support.

Emphasis on Training

Training is an important component of development aid not only because self-sufficiency in manpower is the ultimate aim of all recipient countries, but also because, in the short term, lack of skilled manpower is one of the causes of the many problems which arise in the implementation of projects.

Donors are generally happy to provide funds for training either in the donor country, the recipient country, or, in some cases, especially where language is a problem, in a third country. This might involve university courses for students, but more often rather shorter courses immediately related to specific professions, since recipient countries are generally eager to build up their own universities, and donors are aware of the importance of providing training which is of practical value and does not involve the personnel in too long a period overseas.

In addition, in aid projects and programmes involving major capital expenditure, donors sometimes include reference to training. Too often this is interpreted to mean counterpart training – a method of instruction by which counterpart staff are nominated to work with a visiting consultant or adviser, and to learn by looking over his or her shoulder. In practice, this has proved generally unsuccessful, not only because the consultant is more concerned with getting the job done than training staff, but also because the counterparts are either not provided at all or are not of the appropriate calibre. It is not uncommon for aid projects to have a small budgetary allocation for training which is never spent, both because donors do not know how to use it effectively and because recipients, in practice, are not wholeheartedly in favour.

Individuals, of course, are generally very keen to receive training, at least if this involves foreign travel, more qualifications and perhaps promotion, but governments are loth to lose staff even for a short period, when they are in such short supply. Under severe pressure to show results, a ministry is unlikely to favour sending its most able civil servants abroad for training — especially as they may change department, or even ministry on their return.

Thus, while developing countries recognise the need for more skilled manpower, they often resist releasing staff for overseas training, especially if they doubt its practical value. One solution which is slowly gaining support is for more training to be carried out in the recipient countries, with foreign assistance. This may involve setting up new training institutes, or running courses within government departments related specifically to their current tasks, so that those involved learn while in the job and can immediately test and apply what they have learnt. This allows the building of institutional rather than individual capacity, and ensures the relevance of the training to the specific context.

At present, total technical assistance (of all kinds) forms a significant proportion of bilateral and multilateral aid (nearly 30 per cent for the former, but less for the latter). Yet the greater part of this is spent on salaries and expenses of foreign staff rather than the training of local staff. This is an imbalance which needs to be rectified. While recipient countries agree on the need to increase and improve training, the short term imperatives tend to reduce the priority that they attach to it, with the result that, unless donor agencies are particularly pressing, the importance of training is in fact ignored. Economic growth and eventual self-sufficiency will be achieved, it is true, only by investment; but investment in human resources is perhaps the most important of all. Yet in terms of total aid expenditure only a very small proportion is spent on manpower development.

Increasing Personal Contact

It is clear to most administrators of aid that many of the problems encountered can be mitigated by establishing an atmosphere of mutual trust between the representatives of the donor and the recipient agencies. The sort of close relationship that is required cannot be built up by those in head office, even if they make numerous visits to the recipient country. It is doubtful whether it can be established even by operating from a regional office. But those donors who maintain permanent offices in recipient countries have at least the opportunity of so doing.

Although it is often strikingly obvious when one donor agency, or more frequently an individual representative, has established such a relationship, it is difficult to say how or why this has occurred. Each agency tends to have a 'style' which is determined by a number of different factors such as the size of their local office, the extent to which they employ local staff in professional posts, and how closely they become involved in the day-to-day activities of the ministries with which they come into contact; but the personnel who happen to staff the agency are always of crucial importance. Mention has been made already of the problems that arise in aid negotiations because of the secrecy and lack of frank discussion that often typify the activities of aid donors. Perhaps this is simply the inevitable problem of bureaucracy, but it is exacerbated when the powers of civil servants are reduced while their responsibilities are increased, without commensurate guidance in the form of specific policies. The solution lies in increasing the power and autonomy of the local representative of the donor agency so as to allow much more freedom of decision at this level, and to encourage local aid administrators to build up a frank and open relationship with those ministries with which they come into contact.

Automatic Transfers

Let me now turn to a more radical proposal, which has been made most recently by the Brandt Commission. This is the suggestion that aid should take the form of an automatic transfer -- somewhat akin to an international tax levied on the rich countries and disbursed to the poor countries.

In order to analyse how such a system might be operated I refer back to my discussion of the aid process and the identification of three major decisions: how much aid is provided in total, how much each country receives, and what it is spent on. Clearly the first of these decisions would have to be taken jointly by the donors and recipients. The second could be taken by the recipients alone, but might have to be subject to some control by the donors to avoid malpractice. The main question, however, relates to the third decision; whether donors should exercise any control over the uses to which funds are put. There are two alternatives; one is that the funds be disbursed by one or more huge multilateral agencies rather like those already existing. This possibility has, in effect, already been discussed.

The second is that the aid is transferred automatically, with no restrictions whatever, to be spent as the recipient country wishes. This would obviously avoid many of the problems identified in this book but there are three major objections that might be raised. The first is that this arrangement would prevent the donors exercising leverage in their own interest. The second objection is that the recipients are not competent to use the funds wisely. The third is that the door would be opened to corruption, both in the form of individual financial gain, and the use of aid as patronage.

Let me consider each of these objections in turn. The first is undoubtedly true and for some or perhaps even most donors this would be a very important consideration. As I have already remarked, however, in so far as it is used for this purpose the term 'aid' is a misnomer, and, for this type of financial transfer to be done away with or reclassified under some less misleading title would be all to the good.

The second objection deserves more attention. It is true that developing countries are typically lacking in skilled manpower and would undoubtedly make many mistakes in their use of such funds. But there are countervailing arguments. First, the technical competence of foreign experts is not invariably greater, and even when it is, the foreigner's ignorance of local conditions considerably limits his or her potential contribution. Secondly, as we have seen, a foreign expert may only offer advice, without having the power to ensure that it is acted upon. Thirdly, this approach can never be a long term solution. Local staff will acquire experience only by learning from their mistakes, and projects will never be designed in a manner appropriate to the local conditions unless they are planned on the basis that responsibility for implementation lies with the recipient country.

It would be naive to assume that no expertise at all is required, and that there is nothing to be gained by technical assistance. But the most effective help is that which is actually requested and therefore seen by the recipient as necessary, and such assistance is likely to be best utilised if the recipient is directly involved in the hiring and firing of the personnel. This suggests an alternative for consideration. In addition to financial aid, donors could offer a specified amount of technical assistance (or the recipient could choose to use a certain proportion of the aid funds in this way). In either case the recipient country would be able to utilise the services of foreign experts in so far as they felt this was necessary, and these personnel would be directly answerable to the recipient country.

The third objection to the proposal of automatic transfers is the most serious. By removing controls over the way in which money is spent donors would lose any chance of preventing corruption. In order to assess the gravity of this objection one has to ask how far aid agencies effectively control it at present, and what might be the result of failing to do so.

For obvious reasons it is extremely difficult to give any reliable assessment of the extent of corruption associated with foreign-financed as opposed to locally-financed government expenditure in developing countries. As Gunnar Myrdal rightly says, 'Corruption is almost taboo as a research topic'.[3] His view is that 'the general level of corruption is unquestionably higher [in Asian countries] than in Western developed countries', an opinion which most aid administrators would share.

But to what extent do aid donors effectively control it at the moment? Much aid is undoubtedly misallocated as a result of the preference of individual politicians for their own electorate, their own tribal group or whatever. And aid donors are often aware of this and prepared to compromise with regard to the use of aid for the direct material benefit of politicians or civil servants; but the various rules and procedures, complex as they may be, cannot prevent much that goes on. The question is whether the extent to which donors are successful in preventing corruption is sufficient to justify the very considerable costs that result from attempting to do so. Why not simply relax the controls and let the recipient countries spend the funds as they will? At least this will save a lot of money now spent on administration and control, and avoid many of the problems described in this book which result from the complexity of the aid process. Unfortunately there is simply not enough evidence on which to judge. I do not know, and I do not believe anyone else knows, the extent to which corruption would increase. But I do believe that this is the only compelling argument against relaxing controls.

Notes

1. *North—South: A Programme for Survival*, Report for the Independent Commission on International Development Issues (Pan Books, London, 1980).
2. *Development Co-operation. Efforts and Policies of the Members of the Development Assistance Committee*, DAC Review, 1979 (OECD, Paris, 1979).
3. Gunnar Myrdal, *Asian Drama* (Penguin, London, 1968).

7 CONCLUSION

The majority of people in the world inhabit what are known as the developing countries. Most of these people are poor, often to the extent of being undernourished and debilitated by ill-health. The remaining inhabitants of the world — those of the so-called developed countries — can afford to help them.

This is the stated purpose of foreign aid. Yet despite the woeful inadequacy of this aid in quantitative terms, a major problem for donor agencies is how to spend what little they have. And despite the sophistication and high cost of these aid agencies, their actions often exacerbate the very problems they are intended to solve.

The explanation for both these contradictions is the same: the aid process is so lengthy, and the rules of the game so complex, that many of their effects are counterproductive, and all of them tend to make it more difficult for assistance to be speedily provided.

The process of aid involves not one but two bureaucracies — one in the donor country and one in the recipient country. The aid process therefore becomes doubly attenuated, and the inherent limitations of bureaucracy become more than doubled — compounded as they are by the cultural and physical distance separating the two.

It should be very easy to spend money. The problem is that in the context of aid this process is hedged about by such a multiplicity of procedures and regulations that it becomes both lengthy and inefficient.

There are two reasons for this. One is that governments have mixed motives for providing aid. Many of the rules are intended to serve the interests of the donors rather than the recipients. The second reason is that donors are fearful of the incompetence or corruption of the recipient governments and therefore attempt to protect their aid by setting up a system which allows them to both monitor and control the way in which it is used. A further complicating factor is that in addition to the donors and recipients there are other parties involved in the aid process – consultants, contractors, and advisers – whose own motives and interests can further distort the situation.

Throughout this book I have pinned responsibility for the problems of aid very largely on the donors. This is not because they alone make mistakes, but because they still control the aid process. It is they who have determined the rules of the game, even though they constitute only one of the parties involved. If changes are to be made it is primarily they who will have to make them.

In recent years a number of changes have been introduced, and many of the alternatives I propose are already beginning to be adopted. But these are piecemeal developments which fail to question the basic nature of the aid relationship. The time for such questioning is now due, since the aid relationship has reached a climacteric. Long ago, the imperial powers could allocate funds to their colonies, confident in the knowledge that the money would be administered by their own colonial officers. Many years hence, perhaps, rich countries will pay international tax as an automatic transfer of funds to the poor countries, which will be at liberty to spend the money as they will. At present, however, neither situation obtains. Donors give aid, but not freely. The recipients have, in reality, only limited power to initiate proposals, and even when projects are approved they do not exercise full control over their implementation. Aid donors seem poised on the brink of relinquishing their control; but should they do so, and will they do so?

They have good reason to resist such a move. Power over the 'macro' decisions, such as what is to be each recipient country's share, cannot be conceded without losing the opportunity to extract a quid pro quo from the beneficiary and risking domestic criticism for supporting unfriendly or barbaric regimes. Control over the 'micro' decisions can be conceded only at the risk of projects failing through the incompetence or corruption of the recipient country.

Aid donors are therefore faced by two alternatives. One is to go further along the road of controls: to devise more sophisticated techniques of planning, appraisal and implementation and become still more involved in the decision-making processes of the recipient countries, while preserving the myth that they merely provide what is requested of them. The second is to allow recipients more control, to make aid more automatic and no longer conditional on the performance of the recipient agencies, and to concede at least some power over the purse-strings and hence over the way in which aid is used.

For reasons that are apparent throughout this book, and especially in the last chapter, I believe the present situation has to change. The practical experience of recent years has shown the inadequacies of the compromise position in which aid donors now find themselves. But it is impossible to assert with conviction which alternative course is the better. I can only argue, on the basis of this book, that the case in favour of aid donors retaining control is far weaker than is commonly supposed, while the case against it is stronger. The trend is certainly towards recipients taking a more active part in the decision-making process, and there has been talk of establishing an 'equal partnership' between the two parties. Perhaps it is now time to make this a reality by genuinely conceding control, instead of simply making minor modifications to the complex machinery of aid.

STATISTICAL APPENDIX

These statistics are derived from information published in *Development Co-operation*, DAC Review (Paris) in 1980 and selected earlier years.

Table 1: Total Aid Flows by Donor, 1970 and 1979

ABSOLUTE AMOUNTS ($USm)

	1970 Bilateral	1970 Multi-lateral	Total	1979 Bilateral	1979 Multi-lateral	Total
DAC countries	5.67	1.07	6.74	15.91	5.85	21.76
OPEC countries	0.35	–	0.35	4.02	0.25	4.27
Centrally-planned economies	1.04	...	1.04	1.84	...	1.84
Other	...	...	...	0.10	...	0.10
TOTAL	7.06	1.07	8.13	21.87	6.10	27.97

BREAKDOWN %

	1970 Bilateral	1970 Multi-lateral	Total	1979 Bilateral	1979 Multi-lateral	Total
DAC countries	69.7	13.2	82.9	56.9	20.9	77.8
OPEC countries	4.3	–	4.3	14.4	0.9	15.3
Centrally-planned economies	12.8	...	12.8	6.6	...	6.6
Other	...	...	...	0.4	...	0.4
TOTAL	86.8	13.2	100.0	78.2	21.8	100.0

... negligible.

Table 2: *Breakdown of Major Aid Flows by Donor, 1979*

Donor[a]	Bilateral		Grants		Multilateral	Loans		TOTAL
	Grants	Loans	UN	EEC	Other	IDA[b]	Other	
USA	2452	1624	373	–	155	27	53[c]	4684
France	2460	326	31	260	–	162	59[c]	3298
Germany	1305	856	139	319	163	365	7[c]	3154
Japan	560	1361	92	–	21	340	13[c]	2387
UK	1128	36	145	250	28	478	2[c]	2065
Saudi Arabia	– 1357 –		72	–	85	350	91[d]	1955
Netherlands	781	181	161	119	1	132	20[c]	1395
Canada	376	187	151	–	40	164	–	918
Kuwait	– 928 –		3	–	31	70	66[d]	1098
Sweden	616	4	188	–	29	96	–	933
TOTAL	– 16538 –		1355	948	553	2184	311	21887

Notes: a. These ten countries account for over 80 per cent of total official development assistance.
b. Including IBRD and IFC.
c. Mainly regional development banks.
d. Mainly Arab aid agencies.

Table 3: Largest Bilateral Aid Donors, 1960, 1970 and 1979 [a]

	Rank			Total amount ($USm)		
	1960	1970	1979	1960	1970	1979
United States	1	1	1	2702	3050	4684
France	2	2	2	847	971	3298
Germany	4	3	3	237	599	3154
Japan	5	4	4	105	458	2387
United Kingdom	3	5	5	407	447	2065
Saudi Arabia	—	—	6	n.a.	n.a.	1955
Netherlands	10	8	7	35	196	1395
Kuwait	—	—	8	n.a.	n.a.	1098
Sweden	—	—	9	7	117	933
Canada	6	6	10	75	346	918

— not in top ten.

n.a. figures not available.

Note: *a.* These figures relate only to official development assistance by OECD and OPEC members. According to the DAC Review 1980 (Table VIII—7) the total net disbursements from USSR were as follows: 1970, US$783m, of which US$606m were to Cuba, Korea PDR and Vietnam; 1979, US$1432m, of which US$1150m were to Cuba, Korea PDR and Vietnam.

Table 4: The Most Generous Bilateral Aid Donors — Relative to GNP, 1979

	Country	Official development assistance as percentage of GNP
1	Qatar	5.60
2	UAE	5.42
3	Kuwait	5.14
4	Saudi Arabia	3.13
5	Iraq	2.94
6	Sweden	0.94
7	Norway	0.93
8	Netherlands	0.93
9	Denmark	0.75
10	France	0.59

Table 5: The Largest Multilateral Aid Donors, 1970 and 1979

Rank[a]	Donor[b]	Amount ($USm) 1979
1 (1)	United Nations	(2,000)
2 (4)	IDA	1,278
3 (3)	EEC/EIB	1,257
4 (–)	IMF Trust Fund	680
5 (2)	IDB	335
	TOTAL	5,550

Note: *a.* 1970 rank in parentheses.
      b. These five agencies account for over 90 per cent of total multi-lateral aid (concessional assistance).

Table 6: The Geographical Pattern of Bilateral Aid, 1978/9

Major donors	Recipients
USA	40 per cent to Egypt and Israel
France	60 per cent technical assistance, mainly to current and former dependencies
Germany	widely distributed
Japan	primarily to Asia, especially Indonesia
UK	widespread, largely to former colonies
Saudi Arabia	75 per cent to Arab Countries
Netherlands	mainly to about 15 'target countries'
Canada	widely distributed – especially to poorest countries
Kuwait	50 per cent to Arab countries
Sweden	widely distributed – especially to poorest countries
UAE	mainly Arab countries
Australia	*c.* 60 per cent to Papua New Guinea and 20 per cent to other SE Asian and Pacific countries
Belgium	half to Zaire, Rwanda and Burundi
Denmark	especially to Bangladesh, India, Kenya and Tanzania
Norway	*c.* 60 per cent to 9 countries
USSR	mainly to Vietnam
China	largely to Korea

Table 7: Total Aid Flows by Recipient, Average 1976–9

Recipient[a]	Total population[b] (m)	Total Aid[c] $USm	Aid per head ($)	Aid as per cent of GNP[b]	Multi-lateral	Total by Source OECD countries	OPEC countries
Europe	120	456	4	0.2	134	311	11
America – Central	109	1,196	11	1.1	321	872	3
America – South	224	762	3	0.2	222	533	7
Africa – N. of Sahara	82	2,618	32	4.1	739	1,200	679
Africa – S. of Sahara	327	4,975	15	5.1	1,440	3,072	463
Middle East	84	3,021	36	1.5	269	1,189	1,563
South Asia	862	3,688	4	2.8	1,177	1,954	557
Far East Asia	358	1,759	5	1.1	378	1,304	77
Oceania	5	716	143	19.4	33	682	1
Unspecified	–	2,046	–	–	505	1,039	502
TOTAL	2,172	21,235	10	1.6	5,217	12,156	3,862

Notes: a Totals are for aid receiving countries only.
b. In 1977.
c. Net official development assistance from all sources excluding USSR and East Europe.

Table 8: *Breakdown of Major Aid Flows by Recipient, Average 1976–9*

Recipient[a]	Annual average aid ($USm)[b]	Percentage by source Multilateral	Bilateral DAC	Bilateral OPEC	Aid per head[c] (US$)	Aid as per percentage of GNP[c]
1 Egypt	1,993	32	37	31	51	15.2
2 India	1,412	37	47	16	2	1.4
3 Israel	881	...	100	0	250	8.5
4 Bangladesh	859	32	52	6	10	14.8
5 Syria	786	4	7	89	99	10.6
6 Pakistan	775	21	47	32	11	5.1
7 Indonesia	630	15	83	2	5	1.5
8 Jordan	590	5	19	76	205	26.8
9 Tanzania	403	21	78	1	26	12.7
10 Sudan	368	28	25	47	22	7.5
11 Reunion	349	1	99	0	712	24.9
12 Zaire	294	31	69	0	11	6.4
13 Vietnam	285	70	70	1	6	n.a.
14 Papua New Guinea	270	6	94	...	93	20.5
15 Morocco	252	17	65	18	14	2.6
16 Turkey	248	31	67	2	6	0.5
17 Sri Lanka	247	28	67	5	18	8.9
18 Thailand	238	31	61	8	5	1.3
19 Martinique	232	1	93	0	725	19.7
20 Kenya	230	21	79	0	16	5.5
Sub-total	11,342	25	57			

n.a. not available.

... negligible.

Notes: *a.* These twenty countries account for over 50 per cent of total aid receipts.

      b. Excluding aid from CMEA countries. See Table 3, note a.

      c. Based on 1979 population and GNP.

INDEX

For Product Safety Concerns and Information please contact our EU
representative GPSR@taylorandfrancis.com Taylor & Francis Verlag GmbH,
Kaufingerstraße 24, 80331 München, Germany

Printed and bound by CPI Group (UK) Ltd, Croydon, CR0 4YY
08/05/2025
01864411-0003